Fractured Journey

A Personal Account of
30 Outrageous Years
In the Church of Scientology

by Chris Shugart

Dedication

It seems only fair and proper that I dedicate this publication in memory of my dad, Al Shugart (September 27, 1930 – December 12, 2006). I gave him plenty of reasons for disowning me, but he never did. I doubt that there are any current Scientologists in good standing who could approach his level of integrity.

The best advice Al ever gave me came late in our lives. He cautioned me not to stage a protest I was considering. He said, "You're not going to do any good with the trouble you'll cause. If there was going to be some good done with it, that would be fine." I've never been afraid of trouble, but my dad made a good point. If you're going to make trouble, make it count, and make sure you have some idea of what kind of good will come out of it.

I've been ever grateful that Al got to read a first draft of this book when I first began writing it years ago. I owed him at least that much for all of the frustration I must have caused. In spite of his misgivings about my involvement in Scientology, my dad never completely gave up on me. And I don't think he ever lost faith in my innate talents and abilities.

Only now do I understand that those talents and abilities were present long before I'd ever heard of Scientology. And those talents and abilities remain, not because of Scientology but in spite of it.

If I could speak to my dad today, I might tell him, "My next book is going to be called, *Things I Learned a Lot Later In Life That I Probably Should Have Learned Sooner.*" I can almost hear him laughing now.

— *Chris Shugart*

Note to the Reader

Scientology is filled with special terms created by its founder, L. Ron Hubbard. When a Scientology word first appears in a chapter, it's indicated in ***bold italics***. A list of such terms is found at the beginning of each chapter. Definitions can be found in the glossary section at the end of this book.

I've started a web page index of "bonus material" with photos and documents pertaining to my involvement with the Church. Feel free to browse through it. You might find it interesting.

— Chris Shugart

http://www.fracturedjourney.shugartmedia.com/bonus.html

Contents

8) Trouble In Utopia

There's staff discord, deprogrammers, and my last days as a staff member
May – August ,1980

9) Falling Out

Heavy Ethics: handle or disconnect.
September 1980 – June 1981

10) Rising Costs

Scientology gets all my money, I get the shaft.
September 1981 – April 1982

11) Religion, Politics, and Money

The decline and fall of the Mission network, political purges, and the independent Scientologist movement bring major changes.
May 1982 – September 1983

12) The Church Marches On

I become an OSA infiltrator, and go to a big protest in Portland.
Jan 1984 – May 1985

13) A Modern Day Crusade

It's the big protest in Portland, and the Church still has trouble in court.
May 1985 – Jan 1986

14) Lessons Not Yet Learned

I try to start a new business but the Church intervenes, and I go to Flag for the first time.
August – November 1986

15) Organizational Follies
Leaving Flag is a lot tougher than arriving there.
November 1986 – June 1987

16) A Lean, Mean, Religious Machine
I become a printer for the Church, and my wife goes to Flag.
July – November 1987

17) Turning Up The Heat
Donations become a never-ending expense. Another bad
financial decision gets me in trouble—again.
Jan 1988 – May1989

18) Lifestyles of the Faithfully Devoted
The Freewinds is launched and I once again get snookered into
a bad financial decision.
Jan 1990 – September 1991

19) Is There a Way Off This Treadmill?
Getting nowhere fast, and it's still costing me money.
January 1992 – February 1993

20) View From Afar
Moving away from the Church's strong gravitational pull.
August 1993 – August 1997

21) Hard Sell On The High Seas
I go to the Freewinds. Not exactly your ordinary three-hour
tour. And much more expensive.
August 1997

22) Second Thoughts

I become an Illegal PC again, and I start to question my relationship with the Church.
August 1997 – January 2001

23) Push Comes to Shove

Discovering a different side to Scientology on the internet, while the IAS continues their incessant demands for more money.
February – September, 2001

24) Wake Up Call

I finally walk away from the Church with a new perspective.
September 2001 – Jan 2004

25) On the Other Side

Adjusting to life without Scientology.
2003 – 2005

26) That Was Then, This is Now

Epilogue

Glossary

References

Subject Index

Foreword

For thirty years, I was a Scientology member in good standing. In that time I achieved the spiritual state of Clear and OT, did extensive study in the delivery of Scientology processes, and became an ordained minister. I was also a staff member at a prominent Scientology Mission in Los Angeles which included comprehensive training in the organizational policies and operations of the Church.

In addition to Mission staff, I did volunteer work for the Guardian's Office and later for the Office of Special Affairs. Between 1986 and 1993 I ran my own printing and graphics shop and worked with many of the mid-management executives of major departments within the Scientology organization, printing their promotional and administrative material.

Through the years, I gave money to the Church for various services, a Mission franchise, and many donations to the International Association of Scientologists. The total would eventually amount to nearly three hundred thousand dollars. It's no overstatement to say that I've engaged in nearly everything in which a Scientologist could possibly participate.

Much of this book was first written between 2004 and 2005, but for various reasons I never published it. It was a time when Scientologists were beginning to speak out, writing books, making videos, and posting their views online. Many of the stories were disturbing accounts that made my experiences seem tame by comparison. But I wrote my book anyway, if for no other reason than it would serve as a therapeutic catharsis for me. It was also my way of sorting out just what the hell happened throughout my 30 years as a dedicated follower. And I thought there might come a time when I'd want to share my story with others.

My estrangement from the Church was a gradual process, but I think I began to have serious second thoughts around 1999 when the Church's war on the Internet was at its peak. By 2002 I was posting my views on a few of the online newsgroups that were critical of Scientology. In the beginning, I preferred anonymity when discussing the Church. Any former member can tell you about the sorts of trouble you can get into by speaking out. I was living a more-or-less normal life and I didn't want it to get unnecessarily complicated. But today, the proliferation of material critical of the Church is easily available across a vast spectrum of mass media sources. It's changed the game completely.

I have no family members who are Scientologists, staff or otherwise, so the Church hasn't much leverage over me. Still, it's possible that they might try to intimidate me in some other way. I don't worry about it much.

From time to time I've asked myself, "With all the tell-all books out there, does my story have anything to offer?" Hard to say for sure. If nothing else, my story has plenty of interesting accounts that the reader will find eye-opening, scandalous, and at times comical. For the long-time Scientologist, many of these stories will be familiar. For those who are less acquainted with Scientology, you'll get a personal view of the life and times of a loyal and active Scientologist. In any case, it might be worth a read.

I sometimes like to think of myself as the Forrest Gump of Scientology. I was both witness and activist during some of Scientology's most defining moments. As the Church grew, it was also gaining notoriety. This was the era of deprogrammers, counter-intelligence operations, and the Guardians Office FBI raids. During most of that time, I was a fervent disciple who took part in many of the Church's ludicrous exploits.

If I've learned anything from my years in the Church, I've come to understand the thinking and behavior of the ideological zealot. These are the followers of fanatical religious movements, extremist political organizations, and trendy social revolutions. They're society's true believers who are convinced that no end is greater, and therefore no means too severe.

Eventually I came to understand that the Church of Scientology was a fanatical movement that had taken undue advantage of its own good people, exploiting them beyond what is decent and acceptable. Even the most noble of causes loses its virtue if you find that your sense of right and wrong has been compromised.

Occasionally, we all encounter circumstances that compel us to make choices based on what our conscience tells us. Sometimes those choices come easily. Sometimes they come with struggle and conflict. For me they were choices that turned into a journey that lasted 30 years.

"Here stand I. I can do no other."
—Martin Luther

Chapter 1

No More Mr. Nice Guy

See Glossary for: *auditing, Dianetics, Flag Land Base, Freewinds, Guardians Office, Mission, OT, Office of Special Affairs, OT V, OT VII, PC, Scientology, thetan, training.*

I was a loyal and active Scientologist for 30 years. My wife and I started our first course in the spring of 1975, only a few months after we were married. Both of us have had extensive *auditing*, *training*, and both of us worked as *Mission* staff in West LA. My wife Susie is *OT VIII* and I'm *OT V*.

In addition to the training I've received in the processes and techniques of both *Dianetics* and *Scientology*, I was also a Mission staff member who received training in the workings and operations of the Scientology organization. I always had an excellent track record as a student, getting through my courses quickly and without difficulty.

As a staff member my record was exemplary. I received dozens of commendations for my work, mostly for things I produced in the Dept. of Promotion and Marketing at the Westwood Mission. I eventually became the Director of that department and for three years I remained a valuable asset.

During my staff years I also did some volunteer work for the Church. I occasionally worked with the *Guardians Office*, handing out literature on the streets and conducting public relations surveys. I even got to study the subject of public relations with one of the GO's top executives.

Volunteer work often involved becoming a political activist. I participated in many of the public demonstrations that the Church initiated from 1978 to 1979 which were a response to the much publicized FBI raids on the Church in 1977. I was also involved in many of the rallies, protesting lawsuits that were being leveled against the Church in the late seventies and early eighties. In 1985, I was among the first to arrive in Portland to protest the 72 million dollar decision awarded to Julie Christofferson in her lawsuit against the Church.

From 1986 to 1993 I ran a small printing and graphics business. A significant amount of the work I did was for the various organizations within the Scientology network. I produced a lot of promo related material, and on a regular basis worked late hours to ensure that I'd meet their deadlines. I was proud of the fact that I was regarded as a "go to" guy who could always deliver. And it's with some measure of pride that I can claim to be the designer and printer of the very first issues of *the International OT VIII Committee Newsletter*.

While most of my auditing and training took place at the various Los Angeles organizations collectively known as "The Complex," I also did some services at the *Flag Land Base* in Clearwater, Florida. I even did some auditing and training on the *Freewinds*, the Scientology cruise ship that delivers OT VIII.

To explain how I became disaffected with the Church, I need to begin with what actually belongs at the end of my story. In 1999 Susie and I were assigned the status of "illegal *PC*." This meant that until further notice we wouldn't be eligible for Scientology auditing of any kind. Susie's sister worked for the FBI and Church policy states that anyone with a current or past connection to a government organization can be refused auditing if it might pose a potential security risk.[1]

■ **BACKGROUND:** L. Ron Hubbard had always been extremely wary of governments and was convinced that they were involved in a concerted effort to undermine Scientology. Over the years he constructed a number of conspiracy theories to explain what he thought were attacks against him and his Church. In a taped journal from 1967, Hubbard declared "Our enemies on this planet are less than 12 men." He went on to describe the conspirators as "members of the bank of England," who "own and control newspaper chains," and are "all directors in all the mental health groups in the world." [2]

The Church's policy on government connections is an extension of Hubbard's paranoid vision of secret enemies bent on destroying Scientology. In 1982 Hubbard wrote, "Time and again since 1950, the vested interests which pretend to run the world (for their own appetites and profit) have launched their lies and sought, by whatever twisted means, to check and destroy Scientology."[3] It's a view that virtually all Scientologists eventually subscribe to. ■

Our Illegal PC status actually cropped up in 1987. Because of Susie's sister's job, the Church had disbarred us from continuing our auditing. But we petitioned the powers-that-be to restore our status. We convinced the Church that even though Susie's sister worked for the FBI, Susie and I didn't pose a threat.

For reasons that have never been made clear to me, the Church revoked that status in 1999. We tried to petition again, but this time it was rejected. Whatever changed between the first and second time was a complete mystery.

I was now in a situation for which there was no official remedy. Nobody in the Church could promise me my status would ever again be restored. There was no technical procedure that would upgrade my classification. Indeed,

Church policy states, "Any promise made by an org to such a person [Illegal PC] or his relatives is not binding upon an organization or its staff..."[1]

I found myself in a new and different frame of mind. I began to wonder if the Church knew something about my government connections that they weren't telling me. Was I at risk and didn't know it? And if I were a potential security risk, what exactly was the nature of that risk?

I didn't have a clue.

In his autobiography, Ray Davies, songwriter and leader of the British group The Kinks, offered some advice: "When in doubt, trust your paranoia." It's not necessarily good advice, but in this instance, I took it.

The first thing I did was start investigating on my own. Were there other Scientologists in my predicament? Perhaps they could offer help or insight. Was there a Scientologist out there who had a similar situation? I went to the internet, which at the time was gaining enormous popularity. It seemed likely there were Scientologists online with whom I could discuss my situation. Scientologists pride themselves on being effective communicators, and it stood to reason that there must be all sorts of newsgroups made of Scientologists who were engaged in lively discussions on all sorts of interesting topics.

I started with the Church of Scientology official website. I sent an e-mail requesting any information they had regarding websites, newsgroups, e-mail groups, etc, made up of Scientologists.

What happened next, or to be exact, what didn't happen, struck me as odd. I never received a reply. Was it because of an innocent oversight? My intuition told me no. One thing the Church does without fail is respond to communications. Handling inquiries from interested individuals is a top priority.

This was a glaring departure, and it seemed my query was being ignored for some reason.

I could have re-sent the message, or I could have followed up with a written query, but this seemed too unusual. I couldn't shake the feeling I was close to stumbling onto something. Rather than press the issue further, I decided to look elsewhere. Using a handful of website search engines, I started typing in "Scientology," to see what would come up. What I found wasn't unexpected: a number of newsgroups and websites that were critical of Scientology. I was aware of the critics we had. And I was also aware I had entered into dangerous and forbidden territory.

■ **BACKGROUND:** Scientologists aren't allowed to read information about the Church that hasn't been officially sanctioned. Both Hubbard and the Church have always believed that outside information is made up of lies designed to undermine Scientology. In theory, if a Scientologist reads this kind of material, they become upset and confused, thereby impeding their spiritual progress. Good Scientologist learns to ignore criticism as if it doesn't exist. Whatever "bad news" they might inadvertently encounter is discounted as falsehood and unsubstantiated rumor. ■

In my case, I didn't have much to lose. What more could the Church do to me? I continued with my investigation and entered a brave new world—one that the Church would no doubt have preferred that I not see. I found a peculiar brand of Scientology made up of a chaotic network of critics, dissatisfied members and disaffected ex-Scientologists. Some were still pro-Scientology in whole or in part. Others were rabidly against it. In any case, there was another side to Scientology that the Church never mentioned.

Throughout my internet investigation, there was one curious factor I'd almost missed. I didn't find any Scientologists who were still current members in good standing. Where were all the real Scientologists? I had indeed stumbled onto something, but I wasn't sure what.

Tory Christman, a long-time Scientologist who worked for the *Office of Special Affairs* before leaving the Church in 1999, had become an outspoken critic. There were a number of her essays on the internet, as well as some videos where she expressed her views on the current scene in Scientology. One video in particular stood out in my mind. She described her exit from the Church this way: "I hit the wall, just like in the 'Truman Show"[4]

I remembered the movie well. It was about an unsuspecting man who slowly comes to realize he's been living his life in a vast and elaborate television studio. In the end, he breaks out of his prefabricated environment and discovers the real world he never knew existed. It was an apt description of what I had begun to experience. Maybe all this time I'd been living in someone else's manufactured world.

As a Scientologist, I'd always been aware of the criticism the Church received, but I always dismissed it as unjustified or dishonest. The Church was always quick to claim that critics, without exception, had hidden agendas and ulterior motives. The Church insisted these critics were criminally-minded individuals who were dedicated to destroying Scientology.

For the most part I accepted this explanation completely—until the day I began to hold critical views of my own. That's when it dawned on me that there might be some fair and valid criticism the Church wasn't willing to address.

I spent a year on the internet, browsing, surfing, and studying "unauthorized" information in hope of getting a complete picture of the Church of Scientology.

Now that you know how the story is going to end, let's go to the beginning.

Chapter 2

It Happened One Night

See Glossary for: *ethics conditions.*

My introduction to Scientology wasn't all that extraordinary, but it was at least a little bit out of the ordinary. I first learned about the subject in a bar, the Bel Air Lounge in Santa Monica, to be exact.

I turned 21 at the end of 1974; a college kid majoring in graphic arts at UCLA. I had a part-time job delivering pizzas for Pizza Man on Westwood Blvd, and one of the guys who worked there was Fred, a 35 year old alcoholic who was an artist now pursuing a writing career. My passion was art, music and film and I saw Fred as somewhat of a mentor. He was older and perhaps wiser; an artist and a writer who made pizzas for a living. And he drank a lot. By all accounts, this was a genuine alumnus from the Bohemian School of Artistic Decadence. How could I not be impressed?

As we sat at the bar, Fred casually brought up Scientology. I knew that there were a couple of Pizza Man employees who were Scientologists, so I was curious. He grabbed a napkin, borrowed a pen, and began illustrating the ***Ethics Conditions***. I felt intellectual and scholarly in a hip and artsy sort of way, as if a Lautrec painting had just come to life.

Fred made a memorable impression and I wanted to find out more. Skip, the assistant manager of Pizza Man, and a Scientologist, suggested I attend an introductory lecture. Soon after, I got a phone call from Barbara, another Pizza Man employee and Scientologist. She said I might be interested in the Communication Course. "You're an artist and musician, and you'd probably benefit a lot from a course that improved your communication skills."

The next night, my wife and I attended a short introductory lecture. The speaker was Duncan, a bright upbeat sort of guy who seemed to have it all together. He briefly went over a few basic Scientology concepts regarding the basic elements of communication. It seemed to make a lot of sense.

After the lecture, Susie and I were introduced to Cathy, a registrar for the Westwood Mission. She signed people up for Scientology services, which mainly meant she collected the money. The two Communication Courses came to $100 total for Susie and me—a somewhat significant investment in 1975 for a couple of newlyweds.

After the intro lecture we got a tour of the Mission, meeting some of the staff and the course supervisor. During break time I caught a glimpse of a man speaking with some students and staff. Something about him compelled me to go and talk to him. For me, this was unusual, as I was neither outgoing nor gregarious. But I couldn't shake the feeling that I knew him but just couldn't remember the time and the place.

I asked Barbara, "Who is that guy? I think I know him." She said, "That's Peter. He's the Executive Director."

I walked over to him, held out my hand, and said, "Hi, I'm Chris Shugart. You look familiar to me. I wonder if we've met somewhere."

Peter smiled, shook my hand, looked me over and said, "No, I don't think so."

Unconvinced, I asked, "Have you ever worked in the psychology department at UCLA?"

Although Peter tried to assure me that wasn't the case, I wasn't willing to let it go. "I'm sure we've met somewhere, I just can't remember where."

What Peter said next should have stunned me, but he had a charisma and a way of communicating that was impossible to resist. He said, "Perhaps we've met in a past life."

That should have caused my jaw to drop, but it didn't. In that moment his explanation seemed plausible.

The best I could do was reply, "Uh, yeah, maybe so."

I wasn't what you'd call a mystic, although I'd dabbled occasionally in the paranormal. While I thought spirituality and consciousness were interesting subjects, past lives was something out of a "History of India" course I took at UCLA; a quaint cultural artifact, courtesy of the ancient Hindus.

Anyway, I took an instant liking to Peter. In fact, I seemed to like everyone I met at the Westwood Mission. I'd found a group of people that I wanted to be a part of. It was the beginning of an adventurous, rough-and-tumble journey that would go on for 30 years.

Chapter 3

Your Friendly Neighborhood Church

See Glossary for: *clear, reactive mind, process.*

In 1975 The Westwood Mission was located in West Los Angeles on Santa Monica Blvd. It had originally been in Westwood in the vicinity of Fraternity Row, a block away from the UCLA campus.

Susie and I were required to attend a minimum of four course periods per week, which amounted to something like twelve hours each week. We had our choice of afternoons or evenings during the week and all day Saturdays. Laure, the course supervisor, was very strict about attendance, an important element in Scientology.

I learned just how important one night when Susie and I decided to stay home. To our surprise we got a phone call from Laure shortly after the time that courses started. "How come you're not here on course?' Laure asked.

I said, "We just didn't feel like it tonight."

What followed was a ten-minute lecture on why it was important that we attend that evening. I'd never encountered this kind of tenacity before.

Laure tried to convince me that it was my *reactive mind* that was causing me to avoid attending. Her resolve was so unreal to me that my natural inclination was to resist. The more she pushed, the more stubborn I got.

Much to her disappointment, I refused to give in. Susie and I stayed home that night. The encounter gave me my first glimpse into the mentality of the dedicated Scientologist: an idealistic person with a strong sense of purpose, who's willing to go to great lengths to further the aims of Scientology.

■ **BACKGROUND:** There's a basic principle that guides much of the behavior of Scientologists. It's the idea that once you're in, you're considered in for the duration. It's an all or nothing proposition. In perhaps the most basic and most read Policy Letter in all of Scientology, *Keeping Scientology Working,*[1] Hubbard explains,

> *"If they're going to quit let them quit fast. If they enrolled, they're aboard; and if they're aboard, they're here on the same terms as the rest of us—win or die in the attempt."*

All Scientologists are indoctrinated with this idea. *KSW* is the first thing that appears in every course the Church offers. Scientologists believe that what they do in Scientology is the most important activity they could possibly be involved in. In the same Policy Letter, Hubbard illustrates just how vital Scientology is:

> *"We're not playing some minor game in Scientology. It isn't cute or something to do for lack of something better."* ■

There's a feeling of self-worth and satisfaction you get when you believe that you're creating a better world. In spite of their overt zeal, my initial impression of Scientologists was that they were idealistic with a sincere desire to improve the world.

We liked the staff and the other students and we liked what we got out of the course. Through the repetitive drilling of the

"Training Routines," I learned how to speak on subjects that might have previously made me uncomfortable. I gained an ability to confront situations that may have left me tongue-tied before. Susie and I completed the Communication Course and were pretty happy about it.

Though we had just finished the course, we discovered that wasn't the end of it. When you complete a Scientology service, you're automatically ready for your next action. There's always a course or auditing level above the one you've just completed. It's standard Church policy[2] that once you've completed something, you're routed to the registrar to sign up for your next service.

For the beginning Scientologist, the goal is to attain the state of *Clear*. Susie and I definitely wanted that. We believed the techniques of Dianetics and Scientology provided a workable means to achieve greater awareness and abilities. Our registrar, Cathy, didn't have much difficulty getting us to sign up for our next course. Her sales pitch was simple. Susie and I had gotten a lot of positive gains from what we'd learned so far. Scientology had improved our lives. There were more benefits to be had.

■ **BACKGROUND:** Scientology can be divided into two basic categories. Auditing is the therapeutic procedure a Scientologist receives in a counseling or "auditing session." Training courses instruct the student how to properly apply these processes. While students can be trained to apply Scientology in the auditing environment, they believe that it has application that goes beyond the context of formal counseling procedures. Most Scientologists apply Hubbard's principles in everyday situations all the time. ■

The Hubbard Qualified Scientologist Course was a little more expensive than the Communication Course, but we were now on a new and wonderful path of self-improvement. Susie and I eagerly signed up.

I learned how to apply some basic processes like the "touch assist," a technique that was supposed to alleviate pain from a physical injury. It's also used to relieve headaches. There were other *processes* too, and they seemed to work. Not only did I feel I was improving my own life, I was improving conditions for others, too.

Besides getting a lot out of our studies, Susie and I enjoyed the company and camaraderie of our fellow Scientologists. It was a diverse and congenial group of people with similar spiritual aspirations. They weren't merely fellow parishioners and Church staff; they were becoming good friends.

The Westwood Mission seemed to run with flawless efficiency, and there seemed to be a harmonious rapport among the staff, and between staff and students. I thought it would be great if basic Scientology principles could be applied to the society at large. I soon learned that most Scientologists eventually come to a similar conclusion: The world would be an astoundingly better place if there were lots of Scientologists applying Scientology throughout the world.

Laure and I speculated how different it would be, for example, if the L.A. police were all Comm Course graduates. It's a vision that apparently most Scientologists shared: An entire world using the concepts and techniques of Scientology.

L. Ron Hubbard articulated this grand purpose in the essay titled *The Aims of Scientology*[3] It begins:

> *"A civilization without insanity, without criminals and without war, where the able can prosper and*

honest beings can have rights, and where man is free to rise to greater heights..."

Lofty goals, but I was convinced they were achievable through the successful application of Scientology. This was more than just a religion. It was a noble cause. Most religions have an evangelical aspect to their beliefs and practices, and it's natural for people who have found something of great benefit to want to share that experience with others. I, too, wanted to spread the word.

There's been much controversy surrounding the life and times of the founder of Dianetics and Scientology. In 1976 I knew almost nothing about L. Ron Hubbard other than through some of his writings. I made my way through *Dianetics, The Modern Science of Mental Health*, with some difficulty. It was interesting, but very technical. I had a better time with *The Problems of Work*. It improved my attitude and approach to the assistant sales manager job I had. I attributed much of my early job success with what I learned from that book.

Hubbard didn't really gain my respect until I read a pamphlet on the subject of art, a compilation of articles and excerpts he'd written as technical bulletins and policy letters. Here was a subject close to my heart, and I thought Hubbard's take was right on the mark: the goal of art was essentially communication on an aesthetic level. This was a significant point in my progress as a Scientologist. I'd begun the process of becoming an advocate and devotee of L. Ron Hubbard.

Every Friday night was graduation night at Westwood Mission, when the previous week's auditing and training completions were announced. At the end of the event we would stand up, facing a large picture of Hubbard, and give him a round of applause, occasionally accompanied with three rounds of "Hip, hip hooray."

■ *IN RETROSPECT:* The Church of Scientology considers L. Ron Hubbard the greatest man of the 20th century. I went along with this throughout my years as a Scientologist. Still, the zealous devotion to L. Ron Hubbard seemed a bit over the top to me. I thought the adoration never quite reflected who Hubbard really was. It was something I never completely got.

I always saw Hubbard in a different light. In 1976 I watched a video made in the early sixties titled, "Introduction to Scientology," in which Hubbard explains what Scientology is all about. He impressed me as an insouciant and salty character. Self-confident to the point of impudence, he seemed like a classic nonconforming individualist. My kind of guy. It seemed to me that all the adulation was misplaced. ■

One thing I liked about being a Scientologist was there weren't any heavy moral codes you were forced into. That's not to say that there were no guidelines of behavior. But they seemed to be based more on common sense than divine authority. Nobody was threatening me with torment and damnation if I wasn't a morally compliant person. For Scientologists, abiding by a system of ethics and morals was a practical consideration that was in the best interest of the individual and the community.

The Church was very strict in one area: drugs. Illegal drugs were absolutely forbidden. The restrictions on alcohol were less rigid. Still, you couldn't consume alcohol less than 24 hours before a training or auditing session. It impeded your ability to fully grasp the material.

I signed an agreement before starting my first course that I would abide by these rules. But that didn't necessarily mean that I'd follow them. In 1978, I smoked marijuana regularly. During my high school and college years, between 1969 and 1975, drug use was commonplace amongst my peers. It was considered, at worst, a minor vice. So I was caught by surprise when the Westwood Ethics Officer called me into her office. I wasn't sure what she wanted. For that matter, I wasn't even sure what an Ethics Officer was.

Because Diane's office was actually a trailer in the parking lot out back, I figured that the Ethics Officer must be a minor position in the organization. However, Diane made it clear that her post was as important as any at the Mission. She said that it was her job to see that Scientologists at Westwood were abiding by Church rules. She added that she had the authority to prohibit Scientologists from continuing their training and auditing if they fell out of line.

Then she asked me in an accusing way, "What were you doing smoking marijuana?" How did she know? Susie must have spilled the beans.

I wasn't the sort of person who was intimidated by people in positions of authority, and certainly not those who operated in trailers. I fired back, "What do you mean, 'what was I doing?' You already seem to know what I was doing." She lightened up and said that she wasn't getting after me because I was a bad person, but because smoking marijuana was preventing me from getting the full gains of Scientology. She said that if I intended to go Clear, I'd have to give up drugs.

I understood that drugs and Scientology were incompatible. And I knew intuitively that if I were going to expand mentally and spiritually, regardless of what path I took, drugs would never be a part of the process. I was struggling to admit to myself that drugs were hindering my life. I made my decision there and then in that trailer in the parking lot to stop taking drugs. And I remained determined to continue my progress in Scientology.

When I got home, Susie was relieved to hear I had turned over a new leaf. Her reaction seemed a little odd. Relieved? I could see how she would be happy, glad, encouraged perhaps, but relieved?

It turned out there was another aspect to all of this that I hadn't been aware of. Susie told me she'd discussed another option with Diane in the event I remained unwilling to give up marijuana. She said they'd discussed the possibility that she and I might have to separate, until I agreed to stop.

That should have sent a chill up and down my spine, but at the time it didn't. I don't think I took the threat that seriously. It seemed unreal that a church would actually advocate breaking up a marriage and hold something like that over your head.

■ *IN RETROSPECT:* I would learn later that many Scientologists have faced dilemmas similar to the one I almost faced. I was fortunate the issue had never reached an ultimatum. It's impossible for a Scientologist to maintain a relationship with anyone who has any kind of disagreement with the principles, activities, or policies of the Church. The policy is simple and explicit: You either handle the disagreement, or you end the relationship[4]. Many marriages and other family relationships have ended because a Scientologist was compelled to make a choice between a loved one and Scientology. Entire families have broken up as a result.

Church officials sometimes deny it or soft-peddle the practice, but there is a "disconnection" procedure[4] that compels Scientologists to sever ties with people who have any kind of antipathy towards Scientology. The practice has created considerable friction between Scientologists and their nonmember families and friends. It also continues to be a major subject of contention with ex-Scientologists. ■

Chapter 4

In With the In Crowd

See Glossary for: *class IV, clearing, E-meter, fifth invader force, implant,*

With two courses under our belts, Susie and I were ready for more. We eagerly signed up for the Hubbard Student Dianetics Course. The cost of auditing was pretty expensive, and one alternative was to co-audit with another student. Our plan was to become Dianetics auditors so we could co-audit through all of the procedures, and achieve the state of Clear.

I had a sales and administration job for a small company in West L.A. and Susie was working as a loan processor for an escrow company. We were getting by, but professional auditing was way out of our budget. The Dianetics Course was expensive enough—several hundred dollars for each of us—plus we had to lay out a few more hundred dollars for an *E-meter*. But in the grand scheme of things it seemed like a good investment.

The Hubbard Student Dianetics Course, or HSDC, would take several months to complete. The course pack was two inches thick, filled with Hubbard's technical bulletins and policy letters. My study routine settled into a pattern of reading some bulletins and then drilling the Dianetics processes which included detailed drills on operating the E-meter.

About a week before Susie and I finished the HSDC, someone named Rick came to Westwood to pay us a special visit. He was a registrar from the Los Angeles Organization, a

Class IV Church that was qualified to deliver a more advanced selection of auditing and training. He told us if we were planning to be Dianetics auditors, we'd have to take the Minister's Course, and after that do the Dianetics Internship. No one had told us this. All we wanted to do was co-audit Dianetics. Rick insisted that in order to be properly certified we'd have to become fully interned Ministers of the Church.

Though it was more than we'd bargained for, there didn't seem to be other options. Since we'd already gotten this far, we wrote out a check for a few more hundred dollars. We didn't think much about the added expense.

Before I could graduate from my course, I had to take a written test. The Mission was neither equipped nor qualified to conduct it so I'd have to go to another organization. Westwood had a standing agreement with a Class IV Org qualified to handle all of Westwood's prospective graduates. It was called Celebrity Center.

In 1976, Celebrity Center was on La Brea Ave. in West Hollywood. I was surprised to find out that the Church of Scientology had a special church geared towards artists, musicians, actors, and the like. I thought that was pretty cool. I considered myself an artist and musician, and I thought that maybe one of these days they'd let me be a member of their group.

■ **BACKGROUND:** Hubbard had always recognized the value of celebrities. From early on, he issued Policy Letters, orders and memos regarding the recruitment and special treatment of celebrities. The Church is acutely aware of the PR value of having famous people publicly advocating Scientology. The Church believes that movie stars, recording artists, and so forth, give them an additional level of respect and credibility. ■

When I arrived at Celebrity Center, the first things that caught my eye were the 8 x 10 black and white glossies of the celebrity Scientologists. It was the standard display we've all seen in restaurants, etc, autographed with "Best Wishes" and so on. Of the couple of dozen pictures, I recognized a few: Chick Corea, Karen Black, Cathy Lee Crosby, Judy Norton and Diane Cannova. Not what you'd call huge celebrities, but I was still impressed.

Some of the staff were dressed in the casual Hollywood style popular in the seventies—sort of a West-Coast disco look. One guy had a 1970's Rod Stewart type shag haircut, platform shoes, and metallic silver pants.

"That's Micky McMeel, from Three Dog Night," the receptionist chirped.

I'd never heard of him, though I knew who Three Dog Night was. In any case, he looked over-dressed.

After I was done taking my test I waited for the results in the Center's reference library, and browsed through some of the Scientology books. There was one that looked intriguing: *The History of Man*[1]. It turned out to be more than intriguing. For someone relatively new to Scientology, it was downright bizarre.

It starts out, "This is a cold-blooded and factual account of your last sixty trillion years." From my Dianetics study, I knew about the "time track," a moment by moment mental chronicle of everything that's ever happened in one's lifetime. In *The History of Man*, I discovered there was also a "genetic time track" that consisted of all of the incidents that have occurred along one's evolutionary line. There was also the "whole track," a time track that extended far beyond one's immediate lifetime. Past lives—that was a new one on me.

Hubbard revealed in this book that we're essentially spiritual beings of virtually unlimited longevity with the ability to exist independently of the physical world. The spirit, or the **thetan** as Scientologists refer to it, has typically existed trillions of years, living countless numbers of lifetimes in countless numbers of places.

According to Hubbard, not only are we the effect of unpleasant experiences we've received in this lifetime, we are also the effect of incidents dating back to Earth's prehistory and even times and places far beyond Earth. In the book, Hubbard described a number of these incidents which I found weird beyond description. Things like the "Ice Cube Incident," and the "Jack-in-the-Box" incident were but a few of the **implants** that we received millions of years ago: forcefully administered discipline using elaborate electronic devices, designed to keep us obedient to the laws of ancient intergalactic societies.

I had no idea what to make of all this. On one hand it was incomprehensible; yet on the other, it staggered my imagination. It was like the thrill you get riding a roller-coaster or watching a scary movie. I decided that I'd go along for the ride. I didn't mention it to Susie, though. I thought it would be too weird to bring up. I did however, discuss these new ideas with Laure, the course supervisor from Westwood.

She said, yes, Scientology does believe in past lives, and lives not necessarily limited to this planet.

I had to think about that for a while.

■ **BACKGROUND:** My encounter with *The History of Man* was only a beginning step towards a new level of Scientology concepts. Much of Hubbard's "upper level" material was filled with science-fiction-type ideas. At the time, I didn't know that before he wrote Dianetics, Hubbard wrote science fiction.

An important policy in the Scientology is to only provide a Scientologist with the material they're prepared to handle at their particular level. Discussing "advanced" material with a beginning Scientologist is called "out gradient." It isn't allowed. Should a student stumble on to something like *Fifth Invader Force*, a course supervisor might simply answer that it was a pre-Earth civilization. But for the novice, such things are never dwelled on. Nevertheless, Scientology does contain some space opera material comparable to any sci-fi novel.

Maybe Scientology attracts people with a certain frame of mind. I can't say for sure. But I adjusted my perspective on the more far out aspects of Scientology. It wasn't that hard to do.

Like Celebrity Center, the Los Angeles Organization was a Class IV Org. It used to be in the Westlake area downtown where Susie and I did the Minister's Course. The course was relatively short, consisting of a fundamental background of the major religions of the world, and instruction on the formal ceremonies of Scientology. As a certified minister, I'd be able to deliver religious services for weddings, funerals and naming ceremonies (akin to the Christian baptism).

I was proud of my accomplishment. Becoming an ordained minister felt like being inducted into the Justice League and the X-Men, all rolled into one. I'd become one of the Guardians of the Galaxy, selflessly dedicated to truth and justice throughout the universe.

Hubbard, whose writing style came from the pulp fiction of the thirties, sometimes injected a melodramatic comic-book-hero motif into his philosophy. In *Keeping Scientology Working*[2], he wrote:

> *"Not one namby-pamby bunch of panty-waist dilettantes have ever made anything. It's a tough universe."*

That line could have come right out of Marvel comics. But I liked Marvel comics, and I took a liking to Hubbard's super-hero rhetoric.

By this time, I was becoming aware that as a Scientologist, I had duties and responsibilities. I was expected at all times to promote Scientology to my friends and family. I was also expected to either be on a training course, getting auditing, or in the process of getting together the necessary funds for my next service.

Scientology was beginning to be an integral part of my normal activities. Because the principles and techniques could be applied to all of life's situations, I was becoming a Scientologist above all else. Consequently, it was getting time consuming.

The Scientologists that I was getting to know were very focused and dedicated towards expanding the Church. Hubbard pulled no punches as to the magnitude of the stakes in this game. In *Keeping Scientology Working*[2] Hubbard stated:

> *"The whole agonized future of this planet, every Man, Woman and Child on it, and your own destiny for the next endless trillions of years depend on what you do here and now with and in Scientology"*

Hubbard would often portray Scientology as if it were an epic story of legendary proportion, with noble Scientologists in the vanguard, carrying out heroic deeds destined to go down in the annals of human history. It was grand theater and I was attracted to the zeal Scientologists put into everything they did. I found it a refreshing contrast to the general apathy I saw in society.

Although I was eager to be a part of this adventure, I still wasn't ready to go all the way. On top of my full time job, I was pursuing a music career, writing songs, making demo recordings, and trying to put a band together. I wanted to spend more time creating and performing music. That meant I'd have to spend less time doing Scientology.

I quickly found out that such an attitude was frowned upon and discouraged. There was no such thing as taking a vacation from Scientology.

After I'd completed the Minister's Course, it was assumed I would immediately start my Dianetics Internship. Though I insisted I had other plans, I was informed by the head of the training department that this sort of thing wasn't ordinarily done. He added that I might be granted a leave of absence, provided the circumstances warranted it. In other words, I'd need special permission from the Church in order to take some time off.

A few LA Org staff members did their best to convince me my plan was ill advised, but I held my ground. Besides, what could they do if I just refused to go along with their advice? Were they going to kick me out?

After some back and forth discussion, and with some regrets and reservations, LA Org relented. However there was a catch. There was an official "leave of absence" procedure I'd have to go through. What the hell, I thought, I'll play along with this bureaucratic red tape—I mean, how difficult could it be?

It turned out to be very difficult. And it was going to cost me some money. First, I was put on a Leave of Absence Routing Form which was a checklist of all of the people who'd have to approve and sign off on my temporary leave. The list included an interview with a professional auditor, a service I'd have to pay for. No problem, I'd recently paid for my Internship and still had money on account. Weird. I was using my credit on account to delay starting the course I'd just paid for.

The Routing Form was an administrative gauntlet that directed me to see nearly every principle executive in the Church. I was scrutinized and questioned to make sure I wasn't leaving because of an upset or misunderstanding. I did my best to assure everyone that everything was cool. My reassurances however weren't enough. I still had to submit to the auditor interview.

With the help of an E-meter, the auditor asked about any upsets or misunderstandings I might have had related to my studies. Any reads on the meter were taken up and handled. For the most part, it went smoothly. But by the end of the process, I had almost no money left on account and would have to pay for the course all over again when I was ready to get back onto the Dianetics Internship.

Before my temporary absence could be declared official, there remained one last thing: When was I coming back? I'd have to be specific about that. It turned out that leaves of absence were only good for a maximum of six months. Well then, six months it would be. I didn't think it mattered in any case. I wouldn't be able to start the course until I had it paid for again.

This was my first real conflict with the Church. I honestly believed that for the moment, I had better things to do. Music was important to me; at least as important as Scientology. For a Scientologist, that's practically heresy, and I was beginning to understand that. Nevertheless, I wasn't willing to give Scientology top priority over a personal passion like music.

■ *IN RETROSPECT:* For the first time, I found myself examining my personal goals and comparing them to my goals as a Scientologist. Personal goals are often regarded as selfish and irresponsible. When you're a Scientologist, you're considered part of a team dedicated to *clearing* the planet. For a loyal Scientologist, there is no other activity as important as ridding all the people in the world of their reactive minds. ■

Chapter 5

A Just and Noble Cause

See Glossary for: *American Saint Hill Organization, Advanced Organization of Los Angeles, Religious Technology Center, the Bridge. Sea Organization*

At the beginning of 1977 I was promoted to Sales Manager for the company I'd been working for, and I was writing songs in my spare time. I actually had an RCA record executive listen to one of my demo tapes, although nothing came of it. In spite of that setback, I continued in my attempt to stake out some kind of musical career.

Though we'd been doing our training at the LA Org, we still liked the public and staff at Westwood. Susie and I still attended some of their public events, and we kept in regular touch with them.

We hadn't yet started any co-auditing program as we'd originally planned, and Joanie, the Westwood Director of Processing, noticed our lack of progress. She suggested that we get some professional auditing at the Mission. Although Susie liked the idea, auditing was expensive. It would cost over a thousand dollars—money we didn't have.

As far as Joanie was concerned that wasn't much of a problem. She said as long as Susie had the desire to get some auditing, finding the money for it was a minor task. Joanie's solution was simple. We should just extend the limit on our credit card. Though taking on debt was something I wasn't accustomed to, the thought of achieving Clear was sufficient motivation to enter into this new world of "creative financing."

■ *IN RETROSPECT:* In Scientology, lack of funds is never considered a problem. It's amazing how quickly a registrar can turn into a financial consultant when you need to come up with money for services. Scientologists are prodded constantly into borrowing money from friends, family members, employers, or credit card companies. Taking on debt becomes second nature. Scientologists are constantly reassured that the benefits of training and auditing far outweigh any difficulties financial liabilities might bring.

For Scientologists, monetary gain is temporal and therefore insignificant compared to the gains that auditing and training can provide. It's a reworking of the adage "you can't take it with you." Spiritual gain, in contrast, was something you *could* take with you, provided you accept the Scientologist's premise that you're a spiritual being with the potential to exist for eternity. For the indoctrinated Scientologist, personal wealth doesn't hold a candle to immortality. ■

We debited our credit card and Susie got her auditing. Meanwhile, Joanie went to work on me. I wasn't averse to getting auditing, but I was up against the same obstacle: I didn't have the money. With our credit card debt extended and now maxed out, where would I find the money?

No problem. Joanie suggested I ask my boss for a loan. It seemed a little unusual, and I wasn't sure if this sort of thing was considered common practice in the professional world. What the heck, I decided to give it a shot anyway. My boss seemed impressed with my forthrightness, but he politely declined. So Joanie and I turned towards a more conventional plan: apply for a bank loan.

Using my 1972 Gremlin as collateral, I managed to get $1,200. Wow! Just like that, I'd entered the world of high finance. Sure, I was signing on to more debt, but I was also getting my first real shot at handling my reactive mind.

I was eager to get some Scientology auditing even though I didn't have much of an idea what to expect. The set of processes I would get was called Life Repair, the most basic and elementary form of professional auditing you could get at the time. It was a preclear's first step towards achieving Clear.

My auditing sessions consisted of looking at specific obstacles in my life. Personal problems, bad relationships, and past upsets were addressed using the E-meter. The auditor would take up one of these areas and read off a list of questions. When a question got a "read" on the meter, we'd examine that particular "item." I would then recall and relate some past traumatic moment I associated with the item. By retelling these moments, I was removing the adverse effects, or "charge" from my reactive mind. Almost all Dianetics and Scientology auditing follows this basic template.

Did I get what I was supposed to get out my auditing? Well, I didn't get visions of Nirvana or anything that spectacular. But I figured I must have moved closer to the state of Clear in my first major step on *the Bridge*. No single process is meant to be the ultimate end-all of Scientology auditing. My Life Repair was one small step. I knew I still had a long way to go.

In 1977 the Church purchased the old Cedars Sinai Hospital building on Sunset and Vermont between Hollywood and downtown Los Angeles. The L.A. Org moved into the new building as did the *American Saint Hill Organization* and the *Advanced Organization of Los Angeles*, which both delivered a more advanced brand of Scientology. Everyone called it the LA Complex.

In addition to being the new home of LA Org, ASHO and AOLA, it also housed full-time resident staff and upper level executives who managed Church business for the entire Western Continent. One could presume these were all members of the **Sea Organization**, but at the time I wasn't at all familiar with the Church's internal hierarchy.

That same year, Scientology made a big splash in the newspapers. The FBI raided the LA Complex and the recently relocated Celebrity Center in the Fifield Manor building (on Franklin and Gower right in the middle of Hollywood). The FBI had also raided the Washington DC Church. Eleven high ranking Church officials were accused of breaking into several U.S. government offices and taking official documents.

Although it was big news to the general public, it hardly created a ripple within the Church rank and file. In fact discussing the incident was discouraged. It was considered detrimental to dwell on bad news about the Church because it could be upsetting to Scientologists. I was reprimanded by the Westwood receptionist for mentioning an article about the raid that I'd read in the *L.A. Times*.

The Church held a briefing for all LA Scientologists in a small auditorium at the LA Complex. Addressing the crowd was Heber Jentzch, public relations director of the Guardian's Office, and considered the Church of Scientology's chief press spokesman. Heber had a charming personality, and a speaking delivery filled with wit and humor. He reassured us that the eleven Scientologists who'd been arrested were innocent of any wrongdoing. He also insisted the FBI raid was part of a government effort to destroy our Church.

Regardless of what the facts may have been, the raid was creating bad press for us. And I was becoming aware of the public scrutiny and criticism that always seemed to surround the Church. While Scientologists weren't completely blind to the criticism, we were supposed to ignore it. Hubbard never hid his distrust and disdain for the press and government agencies. In his view, they were driven by political and moneyed interests, all part of a covert plan to infiltrate, undermine, and subvert the Church.

In a Policy Letter titled, "Press Policy"[1] Hubbard claimed to know the hidden agenda of the news media:

> *"The reporter who comes to you, all smiles and withholds, "wanting a story", has an AMA [American Medical Association] instigated release in his pocket...The story he will write has already been outlined by a sub-editor from old clippings and AMA releases."*

Hubbard thought all reporters were "sick and cynical," and were "told what to write." He even believed a reporter would "sell out the human race if his editor told him to."[1]

The Church always seemed to be in the middle of some controversy or another. I had no trouble with that fact. I knew that religious persecution was as old as history, so I regarded our current battles as just another story in the long chronology of unconventional, unorthodox religious groups who were going against the grain of the status-quo establishment.

Did people see Scientologists as kooks and oddballs? Hey, I was an artist and musician. To me, that kind of label was practically a compliment. I also had a subversive streak, a by-product of growing up in the Sixties. So I often found myself at odds with the established political and social conventions of society. The fact that the Federal Government was suspicious of Scientology was hardly a condemnation in my mind. And I wasn't about to let the government dictate what I could or could not believe in.

What splendid irony! It was the FBI, not L. Ron Hubbard, that strengthened my resolve to remain a steadfast Scientologist. For me, Scientology was becoming more than a religion. It was also turning into a rebellion against what I saw as an authoritarian and bureaucratic society.

Throughout 1977 I pursued my musical ambitions. I also landed an advertising job for a retail record distributor. The advertising gig lasted a little over six months, and I found myself once again peddling songs and trying to get a band together. I'd also returned, part time, to the job I originally had in West L.A.

One day, Joanie called me from Westwood and told me the Deputy Executive Director wanted to see me. I had a pretty good idea what he wanted to talk about. There'd been some overtures made by a few Westwood staff about Susie and me becoming staff members. Nothing ever came of it, but now Dan, the Deputy ED was going to take a shot at me.

My current situation wasn't all that impressive. For two years I'd been trying to break into the music business with nothing to show for it, while working at a part time job I knew wasn't going anywhere. The words of L. Ron Hubbard were foremost in my mind:

> *"When somebody enrolls, consider he or she has joined up for the duration of the universe—never permit an "open-minded approach. If they're going to quit let them quit fast. If they enrolled, they're aboard; and if they're aboard, they're here on the same terms as the rest of us—win or die in the attempt"* [2]

■ **IN RETROSPECT:** The Church of Scientology has its own apocalypse scenario. Hubbard once stated that Earth had a mere handful of years left before it would suffer catastrophic destruction. Many Scientologists are aware of the statement and use it to impress upon others the gravity of the work they're involved in.

Following the events of 9/11, David Miscavige, Chairman of the Board of the ***Religious Technology Center***, and de-facto leader of the Church wrote:

> *"Bluntly, we are the only people of Earth who can reverse the decline, and we do not have an endless amount of time to pull it off. Every sector of Scientology activity plays a vital role that must be fulfilled."[3]* ■

I wanted to make the world a better place and I saw Scientology as the only option. I couldn't envision a future world of peace and prosperity without Scientology being an integral part of it.

I had a discussion with Dan about my future and the future of Scientology. He then handed me over to Sonia, Westwood's official recruiter. As we talked, I began warming to the idea of joining the Mission staff. But I told her that before I made any commitments, I wanted to talk it over with my wife. Sonia discouraged me from doing that, saying it was vital that I make such an important decision entirely on my own. It didn't occur to me that my decision was already being influenced by the person sitting across from me. In a moment of noble self-sacrifice, I decided to become a staff member at Westwood Mission.

I didn't know I had it in me. Neither did my wife.

When I broke the news to Susie, she didn't take it in good cheer, miffed that I hadn't discussed it with her beforehand.

And she had another objection that I couldn't refute. Scientology staff members make very little money. In Scientology organizations, staff get paid based on something called a "proportionate pay plan," which means that salaries vary based on weekly income. It's usually not much.

Working for a Scientology organization is like volunteer work, though it wasn't about the money, anyway. I was part of the great crusade to clear Earth, and to rid people of their reactive minds. Besides, I'd only agreed to be on staff part time in the evenings. I still had my part time job in West L.A., and Susie had her loan processing job.

Susie finally acquiesced to my grand purpose. What choice did she have? My mind was made up.

Before I signed on to staff, Susie and I took a short vacation. I had time to reflect on my decision to become a professional Scientologist. I had ambivalent feelings. Here I was, setting aside personal ambitions for the sake of a greater cause. On one hand I felt I was giving something up—dreams, aspirations, and my whole life as I'd known it. On the other hand, I believed I was doing the right thing, that I was answering a higher call. Maybe I was experiencing what men go through when they enlist in the army to defend their country. I had reservations, but it felt like a noble and selfless act. One thing I knew for sure: I was leaving my old life behind.

Chapter 6

It's a Tough Job, But...

In the Fall of 1977, I began my tour of duty at Westwood Mission. I went through the standard staff orientation procedure: I did a couple of courses on how Scientology organizations function and operate, studying material compiled from Hubbard's basic policies on management. Hubbard had taken great pains to organize his Church, issuing volumes of administrative policies that covered every aspect of running the Churches. Over the years, thousands of Policy Letters were published, all regarded as gospel when it came to any Scientology organization.

I thought he had a pretty good take on management and administration and that his PLs could be successfully applied to any organization or business. In fact, many Scientologists use Hubbard's organization policies to run their own non-Church businesses.

Westwood Mission had a reputation for being one of the best organizations within the Mission network, and its success was attributed to the management of its Mission Holder, Peter. The sense of enthusiasm was easy to connect with. Most of the time things happened the way they were supposed to happen, jobs got done that needed to be done, and even when something required an extra push, it was done with a light touch. All in all, it was a pretty good place to work, in spite of the fact that nobody was making much money.

I was put into Division 6, sometimes referred to as the Public Division, which as the name implies, dealt with the general public. Our job was to get new people into the Mission to sign up for Scientology services. The Mission had about twenty-five staff members, and everyone had a specific position and function. Staff members were responsible for their own small part of the overall production of the organization, which was always something tangible, quantifiable, and something you could monitor on a graph. The Church calls it "management by statistics."

I was posted as the Success Officer. If someone had done exceptionally well on a course, or had a remarkable experience during an auditing session, it was my job to get these people to write up the details. We called them "success stories" and we'd post them on a couple of bulletin boards to show the glowing results achieved in Scientology.

In the beginning, I performed pretty well. My graph was on a six week upward trend as I managed each week to extract more success stories than the week before. But I finally reached a saturation point. There were only so many people doing a finite amount of services. I couldn't keep my stats up week after week indefinitely. But that didn't matter within the context of Hubbard's management policies. All staff members are expected to get their stats up every week without exception. In Scientology, up is up, down is down, regardless of circumstances. There are no excuses, just results.

■ **BACKGROUND:** One of the most applied principles in Scientology are the Ethics Conditions. They're a series of detailed formulas used to remedy poor production and enhance and maintain good production. When a Scientologist's production stats are down, there's a corresponding step-by-step formula to get the stat back up. If one's stats are up, you use the appropriate formula to keep those stats up. Not only do staff members use the Ethics Conditions in their jobs, but public Scientologists use them as well in their personal activities. ■

By the end of 1977, my boss at my "paying" part-time job had to fire me. We had a good relationship and he liked my work, but the company was expanding. He needed me to work full time, and since I wasn't willing to do that, I had to go. Now, with my time freed up, I decided I could sign a full time two-and-half-year contract with Westwood Mission.

Full-time staff put in long hours in all Scientology organizations. I'm amazed at how easily I fell into the regimen, since I never considered myself exceptionally industrious.

I worked six days a week, usually eleven hours a day. Study time ran from 9:30 AM to noon. Production time was from 1-10:30 PM with an hour for dinner. On Saturdays I worked from 10:00 AM to 6:00 PM with an hour for lunch. I was working 72 hours a week, and that was just during an ordinary week. Sometimes I'd put in extra hours, usually to get my stats up. It's par for the course if you're full time staff in any Scientology organization.

In 1978, I was still in Division 6, involved in a variety of duties besides soliciting "success stories." During the day, a handful of us would sell the *Dianetics* book to strangers on the street. Sometimes people would actually buy one. It was only four dollars.

Our sales approach was straightforward. We'd walk up to people, introduce ourselves and tell them that *Dianetics the Modern Science of Mental Health*, by L. Ron Hubbard was a book about the mind—*your mind*. It explained why people think and behave the way they do. Over time, I managed to sell a few books. Once, while riding a Santa Monica city bus, I sold a book to the bus driver.

In Scientology, someone who buys *Dianetics* is then designated a "book buyer," a particular category of Scientology public. After selling a book, I was supposed to get the buyer's name, address and phone number. I'd explain to the buyer that the Mission might want to follow up, once the book was read, to see if they had any questions or wanted more information.

The Dianetics book was one of the principle ways we got people into Scientology. Book buyers were kept on file, and sometimes we'd send them flyers promoting seminars and other introductory services. Sometimes Div. 6 staff would call and invite them to come in and start a service. Every now and then you might get an angry reaction, but you also got people who were interested in learning more.

Another method was called "body routing." Staff would comb the streets of West L.A., trying to convince people to drop everything and come to the Mission. It wasn't that effective, but sometimes you'd find someone who had nothing better to do.

Our best means of generating interest was getting prospects to fill out a "personality test" called the Oxford Capacity Analysis test. In Scientology it's considered the authoritative gauge for measuring individual potential. It consists of 200 questions designed to analyze ten basic categories of personality characteristics. Not only are new public given this test, even long-time Scientologists are required to take the test every time they begin a new auditing level.

We also mailed them out regularly. Typically, the person would fill out the test and send it in. Someone at the Mission would score it, call the prospect, and ask him or her to come in to get the results. This was always done in person, never over the phone.

The test evaluator would present the results in the form of a graph indicating both strong and weak points. Of course, the weak points are what mattered, because it was Dianetics and Scientology that could successfully address those undesirable areas.

Once the evaluation is complete, the next step is to get the person to sign up for a course. The test evaluator turns the person over to a registrar who tries to sell the prospect a Scientology service, usually an introductory course. The sales pitch is pretty standard. The reg points at the low points on the personality graph and asks the prospect, "Are these undesirable traits things that you'd like to improve?" Whatever the new prospect says they might want to improve, the response is always, "Scientology can handle that."

The personality test was our most effective tool for getting new public into the Mission. For about an hour every day, we'd distribute them all over West L.A. and Santa Monica, putting hundreds on car windshields in parking lots and in parking structures. Sometimes we'd get chased off the premises by a security guard, because technically it was trespassing (there were city ordinances against distributing literature on public property). In spite of all that, we continued the practice for a while, trying to be as discreet as possible.

The executive in charge of our division put an end to our excursions after he heard about our repeated run-ins with authorities. Breaking the law was strictly against policy. For a while we distributed personality tests door to door, but that proved to be inefficient. Despite our efforts, we couldn't come near the numbers we got before. This called for a new plan, and I was assigned to be in charge of it.

I was given a new post: Test Outflow Officer. I immediately stepped up our mailing efforts and started sending out thousands of tests every week.

Westwood had a small printing press that was used to print the tests and a variety of other promotional material. We even had an industrial quality folding machine that I learned to operate. I worked with the printer, Frank who printed the tests for me to fold. We got along well, and became good friends. First I would fold the ten thousand 11 x 17 sheets down to mailing size. Then I'd go downtown to pick up the address labels from a mailing company. I'd apply the labels to the tests with a simple but ingenious hand-operated machine that cut, glued, and placed the addresses on the tests. Every Friday, I'd go downtown to the main post office and deliver the sacks of bulk mail.

When completed tests came in, they came to me first. I'd note the zip code and keep a tally of where tests were coming from. Eventually I compiled a list that indicated which zip codes produced the best returns.

1978 was a turbulent year for the Church of Scientology. The FBI raids of 1977 had resulted in legal proceedings for the 11 arrested Church executives, and pretrial hearings were now taking place at the L.A. County Courthouse. The Guardians Office was organizing a series of demonstrations in show of support for the arrested members and hopefully create public sympathy for the Church.

Scientologists throughout Southern California were pressed into duty to defend their faith. In our view, we'd been targeted by government agencies to undermine and destroy our Church. It was time to take a stand.

I'd never been a political activist in spite of the politically charged times in which I'd grown up. Although protest demonstrations during the sixties were a prominent feature of my generation, I'd never once carried a protest sign about anything. Now I was going to get my chance.

A number of Westwood staff took time off their regular duties to take part in the demonstrations. During the initial court hearings, hundreds of Scientologists marched around the L.A. County Courthouse, carrying large picket signs. It was well organized, and went on for days. For extra dramatic effect we even staged a 24-hour vigil on the eve of an important court judgment. Throughout the night, we silently marched around the courthouse, and when morning arrived, there was a big public rally in the downtown park.

Scientologists were asked to wear ministerial garb, if possible. When I became an ordained minister, I went out and bought a minister's shirt complete with white collar. I also bought a large sterling silver Scientology cross to wear around my neck. It looks similar to those worn by Christian clergy, but has four smaller additional points between the four main ones.

One afternoon I went downtown with another Westwood staffer, both of us decked out in our minister's outfits. We had to park some distance from the courthouse, and walk about a mile to where the action was. We found ourselves walking straight through downtown's skid row, an area most people would try to avoid. I gradually became aware of an aura surrounding us. People were stepping out of our way and standing dead in their tracks to watch us pass.

Then it dawned on me: We were dressed as ministers. Scores of grim casualties of humanity watched us pass as if they were witnessing a religious procession. I wasn't sure what to make of the attention we were getting. I noticed one man huddled in a doorway, drinking a bottle of booze concealed in a paper bag. He looked up at us, and his face brightened, as he gave us a friendly greeting, "Hola, Padres." He looked as if he'd just been blessed.

At that moment I realized that we were probably the only hope most of these people had. As "men of God," we represented a last refuge for people who had nothing left to hang on to. If I hadn't experienced it first hand, I would have considered a moment like that maudlin. But I couldn't dismiss what had happened. I'd been indelibly impressed with the responsibility we all share towards our fellow man.

By the Fall of 1978, Frank, our printer, was transferred to another division of the Mission, and I was reassigned to his printing position. After a two-week crash course I was off and running. Fortunately, I'm a fast learner, have a good mechanical aptitude, and had an affinity for graphic arts production. I was now working in Division 2 in the Department of Promotion and Publications.

Internal Printing Officer turned out to be a great job. My duties and responsibilities were well defined and specific. And I had my own exclusive office, in a manner of speaking. It was a garage. The Mission, in addition to its main building, occupied a two-bedroom apartment unit across the alley in back that included two one-car garages. One garage was the mimeo office; the other was for the printing office.

The apartment was used by our administrative staff and housed the Mission's central files. It was also a convenient place for staff to hang out during their off time. Many staffers would take advantage of the kitchen to make lunch or dinner.

Though I was now working in a garage, I liked it. It was like having my own little company. The first thing I did was redecorate the place. Because the Printing Office wasn't a public area, I figured I had a lot of latitude on how it could look. Besides, it was just a garage—anything would probably be an improvement. By the time I'd finished tacking various odds and ends all over the walls, it almost looked like my old college dorm room.

Some of the staff seemed to appreciate my eccentric initiative. Others reacted in mild disapproval as if I were somehow getting away with something. Peter finally came in for a casual inspection. He raised an eyebrow, looked at me in a scrutinizing way and cautiously remarked, "Well...OK." He wasn't impressed, but I guess he'd decided to humor my indulgence.

The printing process can get pretty loud. I brought in a radio and hooked it up to a large hi-fi speaker. Out there in the garage, I was listening to my favorite music, blaring over the noise of the printing press, and not disturbing a soul. I occasionally borrowed a little black and white TV from a fellow staffer. On Saturdays, I could watch college basketball games while I worked. And for extra comfort, I had a portable heater for when it got cold in the evening. I felt like the boss of my own printing company.

Out there in the garage, I was pretty much on my own. I could come and go as I pleased without anyone noticing. Being across the alley away from the main building, many staffers might not see me for hours, sometimes even days. I started showing up a little later in the morning and nobody seemed to notice. I'd leave early on Thursday evenings so I could go home and watch UCLA basketball games. It never turned into a problem. As long as I delivered consistently good quality printing, on time without exception, no one had reason to question or complain.

Westwood had a fully functioning HGC (Hubbard Guidance Center) that provided auditing to our public. We had two full time auditors, one part time, and a certified case supervisor. We also delivered what was then called the Hubbard Student Dianetics Course. A few of the staff received Dianetics auditing from student auditors. I got a few dozen hours' worth of auditing from an "intern" who needed to log in a large chunk of auditing time in order to get her professional certification. I attested to the state of Clear as a result.

■ IN RETROSPECT: Looking back, my first couple of years as a Church staff member were good times. The Westwood Mission was staffed by a great group of people, and I liked both the staff and the public. We were a tight knit community pretty much doing our own thing.

At the time, I was scarcely aware of the overall hierarchy of the Scientology organization, which was worldwide in scope and took an active part in the management of all of the Churches and Missions. As the Mission Holder, Peter was a good executive and a good leader. He always got the utmost respect and performance from all of the staff. I don't recall a single instance where upper level Church management ever had to intervene.

Most anyone in Scientology during the seventies can tell you that the Missions were more autonomous than they are today. Consequently, they were much more prosperous, and their staff usually made more money than those who worked in the upper Church orgs. The Mission network was much more vital back then. For example, they used to hold big conventions and rallies where hundreds of staff would get together and celebrate their successes and make idealistic plans for the future. They were elaborate productions with lots of music and entertainment.

For reasons I couldn't explain, the management of the Missions changed. In the eighties, strict top-down management was installed that was inflexible and militaristic. A number of Missions lost some of their assets and much of their autonomy. In some cases Mission Holders lost their franchises completely. The Mission network never recovered from this rigid style of authority. And more important, the Missions were never as much fun again. ■

My cushy job at Westwood Mission lasted almost a year. Now that I'd mastered the printing operation, I wanted to become head of the department, Director of Promotion and Publications. I already had some experience in graphic design and advertising. Since no one was holding that position, it seemed like a perfect fit. And the Promotion office just happened to be in one of the apartment bedrooms mere yards away from my printing office. I was promoted and everything seemed to be looking up.

Early in 1979, Peter had created the PRO Unit, which was short for Public Relations Office. It was supposed to be an executive committee established to handle public relations with the West L.A. community, oversee Westwood promotional material, and improve the image of the Mission. The exec in charge was Peter's wife, Lisa.

She was charismatic like Peter, but in a different way. Lisa was like an enigma from a different time and place. She operated with an air of royalty, as if her power was derived from the divine right of kings. I wasn't the only one who noticed. Behind her back, some staff members referred to Lisa as "her royal highness." Her aristocratic demeanor may have been her only talent. She seemed knowledgeable of very little, and never demonstrated any expertise in anything.

I liked Peter a lot, and I did my best to get along with Lisa. The two of them seemed like such a perfect couple. Part of that may have been a self-conscious effort on their part. I don't think it was a coincidence that they drove matching cars—two Cadillac convertibles. Peter's was white, Lisa's was red. When they were in their cars, they looked like a couple of glad-handing TV evangelists.

The establishment of the PRO Unit marked the beginning of the season of my discontent as a Westwood staff member.

There were three of them, always together with clipboards in hand, conducting "inspections" of the Mission. It seemed like they should have had something better to do. I thought the whole thing was a waste of time. Though I didn't like it, I didn't know what to do about it other than figure out a way to work with them—or maybe work around them.

Chapter 7

Occupational Stress

In the summer of 1979, International Management reorganized the organization board that all Churches and Missions used. My department changed slightly, becoming the Department of Promotion and Marketing. Pretty minor compared to what else was happening.

One new policy put all of Scientology in a state of flux. Hubbard issued a directive titled "The Solution to Inflation."[1] Starting immediately, all prices, be it auditing, training or books, were going to go up. Rather than raise the prices in one big jump, the plan was to raise them 5% at a time—each month until further notice. By any standards this was an extreme measure. I thought that the constant price increases were sure to cause a financial strain on our public.

With the new pricing policy came a new sales and marketing strategy. "Buy Now" became the slogan for everything Scientology offered. Registrars urged their public to pay in advance for as many services as possible in order to avoid the price increases. Some staff were concerned about how the new pricing policy would affect the income of our Mission.

1979 signaled another change. Westwood Mission had outgrown the current premises and we needed larger quarters. A search for a larger building resulted in an interesting find: The new place we'd chosen had previously been a mortuary. Before moving in, some unusual renovations would have to be done.

As relocation was getting underway, the PRO Unit issued a memo to all staff. We were informed that all office areas were to be kept clean and presentable at all times, and all staff were to be appropriately dressed and groomed. Of course, the PRO Unit would be the final judge and arbiter of what would be acceptable.

I had no problem with neatness, but the PRO Unit's arbitrary restrictions and requirements were total overkill. It really rubbed me the wrong way. I wasn't sure if I was going to be able to work under the expanding authority of this new regime of fashion. I began to wonder about my future at Westwood Mission.

The Mission move went on as scheduled, and I thought the new environment would bring with it future expansion. In the big picture, I thought that things were looking up, and I was optimistic. But to my disappointment, the Mission never took off.

Westwood Mission was beginning to suffer from a lack of income. We didn't have a lot of public coming in paying for services. To make things worse, there was an undercurrent of dissatisfaction developing that was circulating among staff. A couple of our principle executives had become critical of what was going on.

In September 1979 I had more important things on my mind. Susie and I were expecting our first child in the following spring. My life was about to change in a way that made any problems at Westwood a low priority.

The demands on my time increased from all directions. Peter began to implement new programs he thought would enhance the overall production of the Mission. Every staff member would now be required to sell one Scientology book per day to either a raw public off the street, a student or a preclear. He made the stipulation that you had to stay at the Mission until you got a sale even if it meant working through the night. The threat was symbolic. Peter never actually followed through on it. In fact, he adjusted the quota to three books a week, which may have been more realistic. But even that produced little result. There were only so many people available to sell books to. The program took on a comical quality, night after night, as staff members would descend on students during course breaks and try to sell them books. Students began to make themselves scarce to avoid our hard-sell tactics.

As part of his new stepped-up approach, Peter ordered my department to produce a new issue of *Outflow,* the Westwood Mission periodical magazine we sent out a couple times a year. He gave us two weeks to complete it. It was a daunting task, but I respected Peter, so I accepted his challenge. The Mission was in the doldrums and I thought maybe a gung-ho project could generate some enthusiasm. In fact, it did just that. I had the entire Westwood Mission pulling for my department as if it were a championship sporting event.

With all of the staff rooting for the promo department, I got to work. In addition to my staff of two, I also had the PRO Unit working on the project. We all put in long hours. The first day, we worked until 2 A.M., a schedule that became the norm.

In several days, we had photos, articles, and a rough layout. Once the text was written, I found a typesetter (a Scientologist) who worked through the night to get the type galleys to us by the next morning. I was still doing the printing, so it was up to me to finish the last phase of production. I worked throughout the night for eighteen hours straight. The magazine was done by the following afternoon.

We made the deadline, and both staff and public were impressed with our feat. All of us in the Promo department, along with the PRO Unit, felt a sense of accomplishment. The rest of the Mission felt good about it, too. Morale had been restored.

Unfortunately, the latest issue of *Outflow* represented only a brief victory. Dissent among staff continued to swell. The PRO Unit instituted daily staff inspections that were even stricter than before. First thing every morning, the staff would line up for inspection. Equipped with a clipboard and a checksheet, the PRO inspector-in-charge, would look each staff member up and down, and check off the designated items of proper appearance. No detail was overlooked. Bras were mandatory for female staff. Even fingernails came under PRO scrutiny.

As the Westwood printer, my fingernails were always dirty. It was an unavoidable occupational hazard, so I was given special dispensation for fingernail cleanliness. In a gesture of liberal generosity, they allowed my fingernails to slide just a little, provided I scrubbed them daily.

Meanwhile, Peter was having problems with a few staff that began to formally query some of his orders and decisions. Critical reports were being written and sent up official channels of Church management. According to some rumors, most of the criticism was aimed at the PRO Unit. I guess I wasn't the only one who had issues with them. Although staff members are allowed to write such reports, Peter saw it as insubordination. And he probably took a dim view of unflattering reports on his wife, Lisa.

The Mission had hit upon hard times. Income was down, delivery of services was down, and the numbers of new public were down. To compound matters, Peter was beginning to get into disagreements with upper Church management. He thought senior level Church executives were mishandling some of our public that had moved on to more advanced services. He even accused those orgs of siphoning off our public—selling and delivering services they could have just as easily done at Westwood. Peter was also critical of how the overall Mission Network was being run.

One thing that got Peter riled up was the recruiting practices of the Sea Organization. Three Mission staff had recently left Westwood to join this elite executive unit, and Peter resented it. At one point, Peter refused to allow Sea Org recruiters to come to the Mission, accusing them of wanting to rip off his staff.

■ **BACKGROUND:** In 1967, L, Ron Hubbard founded the Sea Organization, the Church of Scientology's highest ranking division. It reflected Hubbard's vision of an elite corps of devoted Scientologists determined to expand Scientology on a global scale. Members sign a symbolic billion-year contract which characterizes their motto, "We come back." It's a pledge to be of service to the Church far beyond a single lifetime.

Sea Org members aren't hard to miss. Their style of dress has a naval look, complete with epaulets, lanyards, medals, and insignias—perhaps what the Salvation Army might look like if they went to sea.

Everything about the Sea Org follows a military theme. They have military-sounding ranks, use nautical terms in their conversation, refer to their senior officers as "sir," and refer to L. Ron Hubbard as "Commodore." They eat together, sleep together and generally carry themselves as if they're combat troops. They also consider themselves individually and collectively the highest ranking and most important people on Earth. ■

Although Peter had a few clashes with the Sea Org, his real beef was with the management of Church operations. He thought it was creating an adverse effect on the public at large. "The Mission game stinks right now," he once complained to a high-ranking executive. "The field is dirty and needs to be cleaned up."

Peter seemed to be one of the few executives who recognized the Church was having a tough time overcoming its controversial reputation. Management barely acknowledged the problem. When they did, their attitude was that it was all under control. From the Mission's perspective, we saw more and more disaffected Scientologists, and an increasing number of the general public with negative views of Scientology. Peter was convinced that much of it was being created by instances of poorly delivered services, and too many instances of mishandled public.

In December, I got a temporary reprieve from organizational pressures. Peter went to the Flag Land Base in Clearwater Florida, and took the entire PRO Unit with him. He told the staff they were going to get some special handling to remedy the recent problems that the Mission was experiencing. I think there might have been a collective sigh of relief, as staff members realized that the top execs would be out of everyone's hair, even if only briefly.

■ **BACKGROUND:** Flag is the name of the most senior and advanced service organization in Scientology, and generally considered the Church's auditing and training headquarters. Exclusively run by Sea Org members, Flag is said to be where Scientology services are delivered with impeccable precision and stellar results. It's often called the "the Mecca of Standard Tech."

Stubborn auditing cases, lingering study problems, and persistent difficulties in applying Church policies were the sorts of things that Flag had all the remedies for. At Flag, you were dealing with the most expert Scientologists in the world.

When Peter and company left for Clearwater, it was my *carte blanche* to run the Department of Promotion and Marketing without any interference from higher-ups. Knowing that I had only two or three weeks before the group returned, I got to work on the next issue of *Outflow* magazine. It was already in its beginning stages, and had initial PRO approval, so I decided I had authority to see the project the rest of the way through.

By the time Peter and the PRO Unit returned, our Christmas issue was in the mail. I received a commendation from my senior, and everybody thought the magazine was great. Everybody except one of the PRO Unit execs. Shortly after their return, the exec sat me down to discuss some of the "inadequacies" of the recent magazine. Although I was appropriately contrite, I honestly didn't care. The magazine was in the mail and there wasn't anything the PRO Unit could do about it. Oh well, it was fun while it lasted.

I still held on to some hope that everything would turn out for the better. Peter had come back from Flag optimistic. He returned revitalized, eager, and ambitious to get his Mission back on track. One of the first things he did was cancel all requests for vacation time over the Christmas holidays. So much for my optimism. I think I was the first one in his office to challenge his stern decree.

I explained to him that I'd already made plans to spend Christmas in San Jose with my mom and stepdad. I pointed out that it would be unfair to them if I were to cancel out on such short notice.

Peter could be very persuasive when he needed to be, but my vacation had already been approved by my senior, and I was intent on going. He implored me to stay. He said the Mission was in a critical condition and he couldn't afford to do without any staff members right now. We negotiated a little, and I finally agreed to cut down my trip from two weeks to one. With my vacation cut in half, I still considered myself fortunate. It could have been nothing.

1980 was a blur of activity full of new promotion projects. I worked furiously, churning out flyers, brochures and other promotional items. I was trying to do my part in restoring Westwood Mission's past glory.

By now, I was attending natural childbirth classes with Susie once a week. She was now working part time at the Mission, helping out during the evenings in the student course room, plus she still had her loan processing job during the day. Neither of us was making any money at the Mission, and our financial situation needed to be addressed. I knew that eventually Susie would have to stop working, at least for a while, and there would soon be additional expenses.

To meet these needs, I took a part time job as a printer for a small shop on Westwood Blvd. Technically, I had to get written approval from the Westwood Executive Council before I'd be allowed to have time off for a "moonlighting" job. But I knew, as did the Council, that this was a non-negotiable demand. I needed the money.

On the early morning of April 16, Susie went into labor. Susie called the midwife, and I called the print shop and the Mission. We'd set everything up for a home birth, and it was going to be a busy day. By late afternoon, we were proud but exhausted parents of a healthy baby boy. My mom had been on call, and drove down from San Jose, arriving that early evening to help us get readjusted.

The next day, we went to the doctor to get the appropriate medical exams and certifications. Everything was in order and under control. So much so, that I decided to go into the Mission that evening. I still had lots of work to do, and I didn't want to have a backlog accumulating. With my mom managing the home front, I resumed my work. I had a tricky printing job to do that was going to take a while.

Intent on finishing that night, I called home and said I'd be working late. One might argue that no printing job could be so important that it should keep me away from my family during such a critical time. But I justified my choice. I was a dedicated Scientologist and a loyal staff member. I believed in the importance of my work and felt my priorities were in order.

Leaving my wife and newborn child in the capable hands of my mom was only a minor inconvenience. I worked through the night, and didn't return home until early in the morning.

■ *IN RETROSPECT:* The dedication that Scientologists often display is more than just blind fanaticism. It's a combination of calculated Machiavellian politics and devoted zealotry. Staff members in particular believe everything they do always serves a greater good. They willingly sacrifice much of their personal lives towards the infinitely greater goal of saving mankind for eternity.

In the words of L. Ron Hubbard:

"We are the hope of Man—the only hope. Mankind's salvation lies within our hands. With our tech and ability we can create here on Earth a real heaven where man can be free."[3]

Scientologists believe that the goals and purposes of Scientology are of such importance that the ends usually justify the means. This attitude breeds a single-minded notion that anything a Scientologist does in the name of Scientology is senior to any other activity. In 1980 I believed this whole heartedly. ■

Chapter 8

Trouble in Utopia

In 1980, the cracks were really starting to show at the Westwood Mission. Two of the Mission's top executives left. One was my senior, Cathy; the other was Duncan, the Deputy Executive Director. I'd known them both since my first days, and I had great respect for them both.

It was difficult to get a full picture of what was going on unless you were directly involved in the conflict. The Church never airs its dirty laundry, even among its own ranks. Peter was reduced to putting a positive spin on all of the discord. To make things more difficult, Lisa was assigned the additional post of Ethics Officer. Anyone attempting to get at the bottom of what was going on was accused of rumor-mongering or creating internal dissent. I did my best to stay out of the way.

By this time I had an assistant working in the printing area. Dave was the Mission's first printer and had long since been promoted to Director of Personnel. He was one of the executives who challenged some of Peter's management decisions and was demoted for his efforts. My good friend Frank, as well as a handful of other staff had been forced to resign because of similar insubordination.

■ *IN RETROSPECT:* To this day I don't know what org policies were applied that allowed the Mission to fire staff members. It seemed unusual if not outright off-policy. A handful of staff left, remained in good standing, and as far as I could tell there was no ethics fallout as a result. "Off-loaded" was the term of choice among the staff, and I'm not even sure what that means. There may be an explanation, but I've never heard or seen it. ■

It seemed like I was no longer working for the same Mission anymore. But I believed I was still fighting the good fight, so I did my best to press on. That, and try to stay out of trouble.

About this time I'd become aware of a controversial activity known as "cult deprogramming" which was gaining considerable notoriety. People calling themselves "deprogrammers" were popping up, claiming to be able to "deprogram" family members from the grip of religious cults.

The stories were alarming: news reports of people getting kidnapped and held against their will, while someone tried to coerce the victim into leaving the cult. In some cases, the deprogramming subjects were legal adults suddenly finding themselves captive with no legal recourse.

This tactic severely hit home at Westwood Mission. One Monday morning, Paula, a Westwood staffer, didn't show up. She was always prompt and dependable, so when she didn't call in, it seemed like something was up. After someone at the Mission made a few phone calls, the puzzle pieces started to fit together. It was Paula's brother who told us she'd spent the weekend with her father. He implied she was being "detained."

Thus began an adventurous but absurd caper.

First, we got the Guardians Office into the loop. They'd handle the legal angle, and advise us on our best plan of action. We were caught in the middle of an affair that was part public relations, and part intelligence operation.

On the advice of the GO, we sent a staff member to stake out the father's house in Irvine, to monitor any traffic in or out.

Meanwhile, Peter enlisted a handful of Westwood staff to be part of the rescue effort that was being mustered.

Our commando operation turned sour immediately. Mark, the stake-out man was keeping diligent watch in Irvine. But his beat up van parked nearby must have looked suspiciously out of place in this upscale suburban neighborhood. Eventually, an Irvine Police patrol officer arrived at the scene. In his initial investigation, the officer discovered that Mark had some outstanding unpaid parking tickets. He was arrested and taken to jail. I'm pretty sure this isn't the way it's written up in the Private Investigator's Basic Handbook.

Phase two of our operation would now entail bailing Mark out of jail. I was pressed into service, along with three other staffers. With cash in hand we headed out to the Irvine Police station. To my surprise, Westwood Mission actually fronted the several hundred dollars it would take to post bail.

After springing Mark from jail, we returned to the suburban neighborhood of the purported scene of the crime. Instead of parking near the house, we'd drive by slowly. We weren't going to repeat Mark's mistake. We devised a more subtle tactic: two cars alternately driving by the house every 15 minutes. We tried to find signs of inhabitants or anything else that might give us some clues.

After a couple of hours of this, the Irvine Police must have caught on. I'd finished my drive-by run, when I saw the other group pulled over by a patrol car, and in the process of explaining god-knows-what to the police officer. I thought about just getting the hell out of there, but I didn't want to leave my fellow staffers behind like that. Instead, I drove up, stopped, got out of the car, and approached the officer. That's as far as my plan went. I had no idea what I was going to say.

The officer asked me, "You want to tell me what this is all about?"

I still wasn't sure what I was going to say. Winging it all the way, I said, "I know these people. Is there some kind of problem here?"

The patrolman immediately got into my face, nose to nose and yelled, "Unless all of you want to spend the weekend in jail, you better tell me what's going on!"

I really hadn't thought far enough ahead to concoct a wild story. But then the truth was probably wild enough, so I went with that.

As earnestly as I could muster, I said. "We're looking for one of our staff members. We're very concerned. We have reason to believe that she may have been kidnapped."

The officer was not sympathetic. He barked back sarcastically, "What is this, some kind of secret Moonie cult operation?"

I answered, "No, we're with the Church of Scientology." That couldn't have helped my case. As far as the police officer was concerned, that was probably pretty much the same thing.

Still in my face he said, "I don't allow this kind of stuff to go on in my town. If I see any of you here again, you're going to spend the weekend in jail. Do you understand me?"

I said I did, and that pretty much ended the confrontation. I guess we all got what we wanted. The police officer ran us out of town, and we didn't spend the weekend in jail.

Back at the Mission, I debriefed one of the PRO execs who'd been put in charge of our inept operation. After I related the whole story, she made a comment that floored me. She said, "You should have lied through your teeth or have said nothing at all." I thought it was an absurd suggestion. I was a loyal Scientologist, but I had no intention of getting dragged away by police in the name of Scientology.

Though our efforts to this point were unsuccessful, our task had only begun. The next day our intelligence operation continued with a more sophisticated plan. The Guardians Office got a tip that Paula may have been holed up at a motel near the L.A. airport. I had no idea how they knew that, but the GO was like the Church's CIA, so I figured they had their ways. Four of us went to the motel-in-question and staked it out for an entire afternoon.

It was kind of comical, really. The GO gave us instructions to post ourselves at street corners in the area surrounding the motel. We set up at some corners that had pay phones and kept in constant touch all day. We reported back and forth on anything significant that we saw. Except we never saw anything. It was another wasted day of grasping at straws. Still, I felt a little satisfied. At least we were doing something rather than nothing.

■ **BACKGROUND:** Dealing with deprogrammers could be a tricky problem legally. In many states, there are temporary conservatorship laws that doctors and lawyers can use to allow family members to detain other family members against their will for a specified period of time. In theory, the law is supposed to apply to individuals showing evidence of "diminished capacity" who might require a medical evaluation to determine their mental competence. Because the laws can be vague, much latitude is sometimes given to the captors, especially when immediate family members are involved. ■

Westwood Mission learned what an ugly can of worms dealing with deprogramming can turn into. Paula's father, a doctor, had hired a prominent and notorious deprogrammer Ted Patrick, along with a lawyer, in an aggressive attempt to convince Paula (a legal adult, by the way) to leave the Church. At the time, she and her brother were living with their mother who had been divorced from the father some years before. It was with the help of the brother and mother that we were able to initiate legal action.

While Paula's abductors went into legal mode, the Mission went into PR mode. On the advice of the Guardians Office, we staged a picket in front of the building of the doctor's office where the father worked. About six of us spent part of an afternoon carrying large signs with messages like "Where is your daughter?" Our little demonstration proceeded without incident, while one Irvine patrol car observed us from a distance.

For the GO, this was a standard tactic. One way the Church fights its adversaries is to create enough public pressure on an opponent so they eventually back down. Another way is to take adversaries to court. Winning isn't necessarily as important as protracted litigation. The strategy is to create legal entanglements sufficient to cause the opponent to give up the fight. It's a tactic well known within the lawyer community. It's also a tactic in which the Church excelled.

On the legal front, the GO was working with the mother's lawyer to get Paula released. Now it was lawyer against lawyer. In an exchange of jurisprudence, the father was compelled to acknowledge that Paula was officially in his custody. However, he was successful in preventing anyone from seeing her.

As the legal wrangling continued, the father's lawyer must have developed some doubts about the case. At some point he apparently decided he wanted out of the whole sordid affair. The lawyer took Paula away from her captors and dropped her off with enough cash for bus fare and some phone calls. Paula returned to the Mission, and the Guardians Office immediately followed up with a $30 million lawsuit against the deprogrammer. The story briefly made headlines in Southern California newspapers.

About two years after the incident, around 1982, I was enlisted as a volunteer for the legal team prosecuting the case. By this time the GO had reorganized itself into the Office of Special Affairs. Their staff was spread pretty thin, working on dozens of legal cases at any given time, so they'd get public Scientologists to help with their work load. Because I was already familiar with the case, and because I was considered a stable and reliable Scientologist, I was ideally suited for the job. I spent a couple of weeks going through hundreds of pages of court transcripts and affidavits, summarizing and outlining the documents so that OSA could plan PR and legal strategies surrounding the case.

Things settled back to normal pretty quickly at Westwood. Unfortunately, normal these days meant that the Mission continued to struggle. Peter adopted a no-nonsense, get-tough attitude and did his best to inspire the rest of the staff to do the same. It seems that the situation had finally come to "win or die in the attempt."

Unfortunately, my loyalty was fraying badly. My dedication to Westwood Mission was now hanging by a thin thread tied to my respect for the Mission Holder. I went along with this new tone, but my heart wasn't in it.

Peter started discouraging staff from taking on outside jobs. He thought if staff were more focused on their work at the Mission, they wouldn't have to worry about seeking outside employment. Because staffs typically work virtually for no pay, taking outside jobs is commonplace. Peter tried to take a tough stand, but economic realities didn't make it practical. Westwood staff continued with their moonlighting.

Susie and I managed well under the circumstances, even with a new baby at home and only one car between us. We'd hired a Westwood staffer who needed a little extra money, and he watched our infant son during the day. At night Susie brought him to the Mission and let him sleep in a spare office. He made a fuss occasionally, but Mom or Dad were always close by and available.

The next thing Peter tried was an all-hands Dianetics book selling campaign. All staff were required to hit the streets one hour each day and go door to door to business establishments in West L.A. I hated it from the start. First, I had to "dress up," put on a tie, and that sort of thing, so I'd look totally professional.

What mostly bothered me was I knew full well we were intruding on busy people who had work to do. They had neither the time nor desire to talk about Dianetics and the mind. I was uncomfortable with the fact that I was basically being an annoyance to the business community. It's how I would have felt if I were minding my own business, and someone barged in and started telling me how to solve my problems. I'd have been irritated.

But Scientology evangelism conveniently ignores this kind of thing. The work we were doing was good and our purpose was great. Annoying a few people is the price you pay for making the world a better place. We had no doubt that it was for the good of all.

Peter organized another project that turned out to be the final straw for me. Ironically, I thought it was a good idea. On Friday, Saturday, and Sunday nights a handful of Westwood staff would descend upon downtown Westwood equipped with stacks of personality tests.

Westwood Village had about a dozen movie theaters within just a couple of city blocks. It was a dense concentration of movie venues that attracted thousands of movie-goers every night. In 1980, the "blockbuster" movie had come of age. Movies like "Star Wars" and "Rocky" proved you could consistently fill up your theater night after night. With these crowds of movie-goers, there were also huge lines of people waiting to see the next mega-hit, sometimes waiting in line for as long as two hours. Westwood Mission figured out how to take advantage of this new phenomenon.

Peter's hunch was a good one. There were hundreds of people standing around, waiting in line with nothing to do and we provided an activity to break up the tedium. We handed out personality tests to anyone who seemed the least bit interested. When we gathered up the completed tests, we told the test takers their tests would be scored and graded, and we'd call them in a few days with the results. We collected dozens of tests every night.

In spite of our success, I wasn't enthusiastic about giving up my Saturday nights, even for something that was working so well. I had a family life and I started to resent sacrificing my one night off every week. I finally reached my limit. After three years of loyal and exemplary service, I'd had enough.

I discussed my decision with no one, not even my wife. A staff member who threatens, or even suggests that he's planning to leave his post is guilty of a crime.[1] Per policy, the proper procedure would have been to inform the Ethics Officer of my intentions and do some Ethics Conditions and leave staff on a formal routing-out form. I was going to have none of that. I'd seen what happened to other staff that had problems or disagreements with the Mission. They had to endure harsh criticism, and ended up subject to Courts of Ethics, Committees of Evidence, and other forms of official scrutiny.

My mind was made up. I was way beyond negotiating anything. After one last Saturday night of passing out personality tests, I returned to the Mission. Nobody was around, so I gathered up my personal belongings and my seven volumes of L. Ron Hubbard Policy Letters and left quietly. The last thing I did was leave my key in Lisa's in-basket with a note attached. In so many words I said that I quit.

Chapter 9

Falling Out

Leaving Westwood Mission was a liberating experience. I felt relieved and unburdened, like the weight of the world had been lifted from me. I had no idea what I'd do next, since I hadn't planned that far ahead. What I did know was that I was completely free to chart a new course. I saw my life, not as something I'd left behind, but as something that lay ahead. Though I had no specific plans, I was eager to explore my options.

It only took a couple of days for reality to set in. I was still a Scientologist, in spite of my disaffection with the Mission, and I was still subject to Church rules and policy. If I was going to remain a Scientologist in good standing, I'd have to deal with my departure in a formal and official way.

There was another complication I hadn't fully considered. Susie was still a part time staff member, working evenings in the course room. I'd have to factor that in with the rift that now existed between me and Westwood Mission. It would have to be resolved one way or another.

One night Susie came home after course with a note from the Assistant Ethics Officer, requesting that I come in immediately to handle my situation. Susie looked grave, as if she were breaking the news of a death in the family. She asked me when I was planning on going into the Mission. I said I'd make an appointment.

As it turns out, Susie was pressured into persuading me to come in. Susie told me that they had discussed a contingency plan, in the event I was unwilling to cooperate. The Asst.

Officer had recommended that Susie move out for a while until I started to comply with Ethics Policy.

By now I was well indoctrinated with Scientology's policies on Ethics, and so the threat didn't faze me much. As long as I was at variance with anything regarding Scientology, I was a "potential source of trouble." Per policy, Susie would either have to "handle or disconnect." I knew that this meant that Susie would have to insist that I either get my act together or she would be obligated to separate from me.

■ IN RETROSPECT: Ethics is often used as a coercive strong-arm tactic. Putting pressure on family members is not uncommon. Personal relationships, whether they're casual or intimate, occasionally come under the jurisdiction of Church policy.

An Ethics Officer has the power to put you in a lower Ethics condition, which temporarily bars you from further services until you reconcile your situation. In the most severe cases, the EO can initiate the process of expulsion from the Church. Once expelled, a Scientologist is shunned by the group, thoroughly and completely. From that point on, other Scientologists are forbidden to make any contact of any kind. The procedure is called "disconnection," and has caused the end of long-time friendships, and worse, has been the cause of family breakups. With this kind of threat hanging over their heads, Scientologists can be effectively kept in line. ■

My initial meeting with the Assistant Ethics Officer started out different than I'd imagined. To my surprise, the Asst. Officer wasn't convinced of the finality of my quiet but resolute resignation. She asked me what sort of objections, disagreements, and other problems I was having with my staff job. I explained briefly about selling books on the street, and handing tests out on weekend nights, and did my best to convey my general dissatisfaction.

She must have been holding on to some thread of hope that I could be recovered. She asked me, "If you were taken off the Book Unit and the weekend Testing Unit, would you be willing to remain on staff?"

I did my best to tiptoe through my strong disagreements with Mission operations. There were issues I knew I wouldn't be able to express with any candor. I avoided mentioning that I thought the PRO Unit was incompetent, and their authority questionable. I discreetly left out that I believed the rash of staff members who'd left was evidence that there was something terribly wrong with the Mission.

I could have just said, "This is a lousy place to work, and I quit," but I was trying to be diplomatic. I really wanted out, but I didn't want to ruffle any feathers in the process. I didn't want to say anything that might affect my standing as a Scientologist.

My situation hadn't deteriorated to the level of expulsion, but I was aware that lurking somewhere there was that possibility. My view of the situation was more practical. I wanted out of Westwood, and needed somehow to restore my status in accordance with Church policy. This meant that I was going to have to follow through with official Ethics procedures.

It wasn't easy for me to lay out the reasons why I wanted out of Westwood. "Irreconcilable differences" wouldn't have been specific enough. Still, it might have been better than "This is a lousy place to work, and I quit." But the Ethics Conditions are specific formulas that must be applied to the letter, and that's what I'd have to do. In so many words, I stated that I'd much rather be a public Scientologist, than a professional one. I wanted to continue my auditing and training, and pursue a professional career, perhaps within the arts.

In a practical sense, my Ethics status had become irrelevant. I simply wasn't a staff member any more. I'd found a new job as the press operator for a small print shop in the garment district in downtown L.A. The money was pretty decent, and definitely a far cry from the few dollars I'd receive on rare occasion as a Westwood staff member. Moreover, the cost of living and raising a family were exceeding what Susie was making as a loan processor, so this new influx of income was not only welcome, it was a necessity.

In any case, I composed an Ethics Condition formula in a way I thought would make a good "sell" on my former associates. The Ethics Officer had assigned me a Condition of Liability, so I followed the steps of the formula. Among other things I had to "1: Decide who are one's friends; 2: Deliver an effective blow to the enemies of the group one has been pretending to be part of despite personal danger."

Part of the formula required I perform some sort of "amends" in order to "make up for the damage" I'd done. For several nights I cleaned carpets, and did some painting after course hours. Then I had to present a petition to every staff member asking them to allow me back in the group as a Scientologist in good standing.

After I'd gotten everyone's signature, I was now officially an ex-staff member, still in the good graces of the Westwood staff and the Church. Westwood Mission was going to be somebody else's problem now.

The problem did persist, and the Mission continued to slide downhill. Peter continued to clash with Church management and Lisa still had conflicts with the staff. In 1982, Scientology Missions International intervened, and called a *Committee of Evidence* on Westwood Mission Holders Peter and Lisa.

The Committee's findings and recommendations were complete by January 1983. They revoked Peter and Lisa's

Mission charter and cancelled all of their Scientology certifications and classifications. That's about as severe as you can get, short of expulsion. And their road back was going to be steep. SMI ordered that they re-do their Scientology training, and submit to a battery of **Security Checks**. It's what Scientologists like to call *heavy ethics*.

By 1981 my life had returned to normal, more or less. Susie and I were gainfully employed, raising a family, and wondering which way our life in Scientology was going to take us next. Susie had a new job in a Beverly Hills law office and she continued working evenings at the Westwood Mission, in spite of their ongoing difficulties. I was working at the print shop downtown which was run by some L.A. Scientologists.

I made good money for a while, but the business eventually turned sour, and by summer I left. With both of us working, our financial situation had gotten pretty stable. So stable, that I convinced Susie to allow me to resume my music career. This wasn't going to make me any money—at least for a while—but I wanted to give it another shot.

We lived in a two-bedroom apartment in Santa Monica and we were getting by fairly well. My plan was to write songs, put a band together, etc., all the while managing the household and taking care of our one-year-old toddler. The arrangement worked out pretty well.

Although I was no longer a staff member, I was still a Scientologist in the complete sense of the word. My deep involvement in Scientology was always an area of concern to my parents, but I'd managed to keep it from ever turning into a squabble. My mom and dad occasionally voiced their skepticism and reservations, but they never pressed the issue too far. After all, I was an intelligent, responsible adult, living my own life. What could they really do?

In the end, we simply agreed to disagree. This is a major accomplishment for most Scientologists. In the event that my relationships with my parents had ever deteriorated to some level of antagonism that wouldn't resolve, I'd have to face the prospect of "disconnection," something the Church would have required as a last resort option. I'm thankful that I was able to avoid such severe measures. Other Scientologists have not been so lucky.

■ IN RETROSPECT: Nowadays, the official Church PR line is that the Church doesn't enforce disconnection and the official policy has been cancelled. It's a moot point because Scientologists still apply the procedure. Enforced or not, no Scientologist is allowed to associate with anyone known to have strong disagreements with anything related to Scientology. It doesn't matter if it's a child, a parent, a spouse, or good friend.

If a Scientologist leaves the Church on acrimonious terms, they can expect to have all of their ties to it severed. Scientologists will no longer talk to you, and if you happen to do business with Scientologists or companies run by Scientologists, they will no longer deal with you. Many ex-Scientologists find this practice of disconnection to be the most distasteful aspect of the Church. It continues to be a major source of criticism. ■

Chapter 10

Rising Costs

See Glossary for: *suppressive person*

With the beginning of 1982, came a series of events that turned my life in a completely different direction. And I never saw it coming. It actually all started in 1978, when my dad, Al Shugart, founded Seagate Technology. He was already a prominent figure in the Silicon Valley computer industry, but this new venture would soon become his best known accomplishment.

In 1980 my dad gave me a few thousand shares of Seagate stock as a Christmas present. It wasn't worth anything then because the stock hadn't gone public. My dad suggested I hang on to it because he said, in a casual way, "one of these days it might be worth a million dollars." I laughed and said, "Hey, you never know."

Although Seagate was flourishing by 1981, I never thought much about the shares I owned. I really wasn't interested in the stock market, and I had no idea if I was making any money or not. It was something I had no influence over, so I didn't pay much attention to it. However there were those who, if they knew, would have been keenly interested.

My wife casually mentioned our Seagate stock to someone at the American Saint Hill Organization, and it must have created an instant buzz throughout the Scientology network. I had no idea how much my stock was worth but I sure found out in a hurry. I got a call from Darcy, an ASHO registrar who told me that my stock was probably worth a few hundred thousand dollars. Someone must have been doing their homework.

Darcy had one goal in mind. He wanted me to sell all of my Seagate stock and give all the money to the Church. On the face of it, that sounded like an absurd idea. Still, I was willing to let Church executives make their case, as I understood where they were coming from. I'd been a Church staff member, and even though I was now a public Scientologist, I was still part of the Scientology movement. Had it been me, I could have very well been just as eager as Darcy was.

I recall one encounter with Darcy, when he brought along a registrar from L.A. Org named Greg. They paid me a personal visit to my apartment to try and convince me that selling all of my Seagate stock would actually be a good financial move in the long run. They reasoned that prices for Church services were still going up by five percent every month. If I were to wait, I'd only be paying more later. They also tried to stress that paying for Church services was always a superior investment strategy under any circumstances. The gains to be had through Scientology auditing and training were of incalculable benefit. For an indoctrinated Scientologist such as myself, the spiritual gains were virtually infinite in magnitude.

Darcy and Greg's last argument was the trump card that every registrar eventually plays. Because Scientology improves ability, it stands to reason that a Scientologist would enhance their skills and aptitude to such an enormous degree that they could easily generate more income, affluence and success. Like most Scientologists, I believed this was true.

My financial situation had no doubt spread like wildfire throughout a few of the Church organizations. One night, I got a visit from an exec who was with Scientology Missions International. He wanted me to buy a Mission franchise for twenty-thousand dollars. Besides the usual patter about the vital importance of expanding Scientology, the SMI exec presented me with another argument. He went into an elaborate story about how high-level Church management had been doing an evaluation of the world economy. They were predicting an eventual economic collapse that would devastate the world's financial institutions. The exec said that it was only a matter of time that money would no longer be worth anything.

Taking this scenario further, the SMI exec said that the only effective hedge against an economic collapse was to invest in Scientology. Scientology had an immense value that existed independent of prevailing economic conditions. A Scientologist was valuable in a way that was superior to any monetary system. Because we were the only hope that mankind had, in the event of a global catastrophe, the world would be coming to us for answers. A thoroughly trained and processed Scientologist was the only person who could prevail in a world crisis. As a Mission Holder, people would be beating a path to my door!

At the time, it hadn't occurred to me that I was getting appallingly bad advice from Church executives who knew very little about finance or the world economy. I naively assumed that I was dealing with responsible people who were top-notch executives who had just as much reliable information as the most knowledgeable New York stockbrokers.

There should be a Scientology axiom that states, "The amount of money at stake is directly proportional to the tenacity of the Church to get that money." In my case we were dealing with what could potentially be a couple hundred thousand dollars. The Church wasn't going to give up on getting their hands on that kind of cash. But I wasn't convinced and I told Darcy that I didn't want to sell my stock.

One day I got a call from Michael, a registrar from the Advanced Organization. He wanted to take his shot at getting my money. He positioned himself as the "good cop" in this back-and-forth struggle for my assets. He said over the phone, "Those regs are assholes. They don't know what they're doing. Why don't you come in, and we'll work out something you can agree with. The other orgs have turned this into a problem, and it doesn't have to be."

Finally, I thought, someone who was willing to see my point of view. I went to AOLA to have a meeting with Michael. He was a familiar figure around the Complex. He had a funny, likable personality and a reputation for being very good at his job. He was also known for performing mind-boggling card tricks.

At the time, I failed to see any irony in a Church registrar performing razzle-dazzle slight-of-hand card tricks while trying to convince me to give thousands of dollars to the Church. He was an OT you see, and everyone attributed his magical skills to his high-level spiritual abilities. I was convinced too. He told me to think of a card, and he pulled that card right out of the deck. It really seemed like something way beyond a cheap flim-flam trick. I thought he was psychic.

After the entertainment, we had a long conversation. Michael asked me what I wanted out of Scientology. I discussed my goals, aspirations, and so forth, and talked a little about my experiences with Scientology. But I still had reservations about selling my stock.

Michael suggested a compromise. He said that there was no reason to sell all of my stock. I could just sell a portion of it—enough to buy plenty of services for Susie and me. He said, "It's your money for God's sakes, you should be able to do what you want with it."

I thought it was a good solution. I really did want to go Clear and achieve OT, and I knew it was going to cost me lots of money one way or another. This seemed like a good plan. But I had to ask, "How much money are we talking about here?" Michael said he'd get with Darcy and they'd put together a service package and present the whole deal to me.

Two days later, Darcy and Greg showed up at my apartment with a stack of invoices representing all of the stuff that I was going to buy. Because it was going to be such a huge donation, they were somehow able to apply substantial discounts on everything. The package included auditing all the way through OT VII (which hadn't yet been released), and training all the way through Class 8, and a number of auxiliary courses. The total came to just over $100,000. Believe it or not, that was cheap compared to what I would have paid at full price. It seemed like I was buying every service the Church of Scientology had.

■ *IN RETROSPECT:* Although spiritual gain is an intangible concept, the Church of Scientology is adept at promoting it in concrete terms. Although no registrar will come out and blatantly say "Scientology will make you rich," the idea is always implied. The Church always publicizes the achievements of successful Scientologists and members are encouraged to aspire to similar success.

Scientologists are always encouraged to pay for services without regard to their immediate financial circumstances. If you have reservations about depleting your savings account, going into debt, selling off assets, and so forth, the registrar will remind you that it's an unnecessary concern. Scientology is about breaking free from the constraints of the demands of material existence.

To a Scientologist, putting attention on material wealth is part of the problem, not the solution. Therefore, by putting your money towards Scientology, in spite of whatever financial liabilities that it might create, you're expressing your utter disagreement with the mechanics of the physical universe. In the end, you'll be a better person for it.

The utter disregard that Scientologists have about their personal finances is seen as an admirable trait. On the other hand, Scientologists need lots of money to continue doing Scientology. In order to overcome the paradox this creates, the active Scientologist is convinced that as they become more effective in life, they can naturally expect to become more affluent. ▨

Initiating a hundred-thousand-dollar transaction isn't like writing a check for cash at the supermarket. Though it's much more elaborate, the complexity didn't faze any of the execs involved. They tackled the procedure with a frantic obsession.

While the amount of money alone might have been more than ample motivation, there was another factor in play: production statistics. Not only did the Church want my money, they wanted it by 2:00 PM on Thursday. Every Scientologist is familiar with the manic frenzy that accompanies the hours prior to that deadline.

Because of my staff experience, I was familiar with this monomania, even a willing participant. I actually agreed to take out a short term loan to give the various Church orgs the chance to get their money before the 2:00 PM deadline. I did this in spite of the fact that the extra transaction was going to cost me additional money in interest charges. I was caught up in a fanatical moment that lacked a common sense perspective. It only occurred to me afterwards that all of the Church regs still would have gotten a big boost in stats anyway, although not until the following week.

■ **BACKGROUND:** If there's one thing that will always turn a Scientologist into an unwavering zealot, it's that last minute effort to get their stats up, even a little, over the previous week.

Hubbard wrote extensively on the management and administration of his organization. When regarded as a single body of work, these writings are known as Policy Letters, or descriptively called Management Technology. This so called technology has been compiled into a number of published volumes which represent the blueprint of all operations within the Church. Even public Scientologists find these Policy Letters applicable to their own companies and other activities.

The essence of Hubbard's system is a simple idea of managing by statistics. In general, when your stats are up, things can be considered to be going well, when the stats are down, something needs to be adjusted. It's an important factor that influences nearly everything a Scientologist does. ■

Needless to say, my dad thought I was crazy for selling my Seagate stock. There was probably nothing I could say that would be a sufficient explanation, but I tried anyway. I told him that prices were going up steadily every month and therefore I was coming out ahead in the long run. Then I said that the Church was giving me huge discounts. The way I saw it, in one single purchase, I was buying all of the auditing and training that Susie and I could ever possibly do. It was a once-in-a-lifetime opportunity. My dad thought I was being scammed.

My mom and step-dad tried to counsel me towards a more prudent decision. My sister sent me a letter expressing concern that my financial folly was going to create an irreparable rift between my dad and myself. Considering the circumstances, my family showed incredible restraint, especially my dad. He didn't press the issue any further, though I think he did come close to disowning me.

Everybody got their money—over one hundred thousand dollars in all. The Los Angeles Organization, The American Saint Hill Organization and the Advanced Organization of Los Angeles each got their piece of the pie. Even Scientology Missions International got their twenty grand. Since I'd agreed to purchase the Mission franchise that had been offered to me, I was going to be the Scientology Mission Holder for the newly established Marina Del Rey franchise. May as well go all the way. I'd become thoroughly immersed in the purpose of expanding the Church.

In all of the excitement, I somehow ended up selling all of my stock, even though that wasn't the original plan. I'm not sure how it happened. Everything was moving so fast that I didn't stop to take a good look at what was going on. I do recall the broker handling the sale saying something to the effect that the best offer we got included the stipulation that the purchase had to be for all of my shares. I have no idea if that was really the case, nor had I any idea if such a condition was at all commonplace. Darcy had hooked me up with a stockbroker and financial manager who were both Scientologists. I figured they knew what they were doing so I was just following their instructions. Before I knew it, all of my stock was sold. I thought, what happened?

After the Church got all of their money, I still had close to a hundred thousand dollars left over. In the aftermath of the financial carnage, that was of some consolation. At least I'd have the opportunity to reinvest. I began looking at my new options as a financial entrepreneur, although I had no idea what I was doing.

It's one thing to be a Scientologist with money. It's an entirely different situation to be a Scientologist with money and have other Scientologists know about it. You may as well be walking around with a neon bull's-eye on your back.

It didn't take long for a couple of young Scientologists to contact me with an investment proposal. They had what seemed like a sensible plan. They were account execs for a reputable investment company and they suggested that I put a portion of the remainder of my money in a low-risk high-yield account of some sort. It seemed like a good idea to me. It was definitely better than letting it sit in a checking account, and the money would be available should I choose to reinvest down the road.

The paperwork was simple and it got close to being a done deal. But I backed out at the last minute following a phone call from Darcy. There was still money to be had, and he had an idea. Darcy proposed that I loan out the rest of my money to Scientologists to pay for their services.

He convinced me that loaning money to Scientologists was virtually risk free. They were trustworthy, and even if they weren't, I had the Church's Ethics system to back me up. What Scientologist would consider defaulting on a loan from a fellow Scientologist when it would mean jeopardizing their spiritual progress? They wouldn't dare, I thought.

On paper, the deal looked pretty good. I'd loan the rest of the money to a handful of Scientologists who would make monthly payments with interest. I could cash in the interest, and hold the principal for future loans. Darcy told me that he had researched this and the whole thing was perfectly legal. I told him to go ahead and set it up.

The paperwork was rinky-dink and amateurish. No lawyer or notary, and nothing but handwritten contracts thrown together off the cuff. But we were Scientologists. Our word was our bond. Besides, we considered ourselves the most ethical people on the planet. A signature on a piece of paper was a mere formality between honorable people.

It all seemed so easy. In an instant, I'd become a financial investor even though I had no idea what I was doing. When I started getting checks in the mail each month, it seemed like I had a good thing going. And I felt secure in the knowledge that I had the Church of Scientology solidly behind me, keeping it all in place.

A few weeks later I got my first sign of trouble: a strange phone call from Kevin, an ASHO registrar I got to know during my financial wheeling and dealing. Though the call woke me up at 2:00 AM, Church staff working into the wee hours wasn't that unusual. But what could possibly be so important that Kevin felt he needed to speak to me right away at such an unusual hour? I could only conclude that there must be a problem.

Kevin told me that Darcy had been removed from his post. He also said that the other registrar, Greg, who helped put together some of my loan deals had resigned his position at LA Org. Then Kevin then told me that Darcy had a criminal record, and he implied in a roundabout way that I keep close tabs on all those loans I'd just made.

Why had Kevin felt so compelled to call me in the middle of the night? Maybe he was trying to impress upon me the gravity of a situation of which I wasn't fully aware. But what was the situation? I believed my loan transactions had occurred under the sanction of the Church. I assumed I had the full extent of the Church's ethics and justice system to protect me.

On the other hand, maybe my situation wasn't as secure as I'd thought. Perhaps in his own way, Kevin was trying to give me a subtle warning as to what might in store. Little did I know then that the Church would bear virtually no responsibility for these flimsy loan deals. If the loans went awry, the Church would consider it my problem, not theirs.

Trouble did indeed crop up only months after I'd started my loan business. One of my "clients" was late with a payment and so I made a phone call. Stan was contrite and sounded sincere about making good on the loan. It's just that he discovered that paying it back was turning into a greater burden than he'd anticipated. Didn't Darcy screen these applicants? I thought I'd be dealing with responsible Scientologists who had their financial scenes under control.

Stan was a nice enough guy, but a little flaky when it came to money. And on top of that he was a musician, a struggling one at that. What was a musician of modest means doing taking out a loan in the first place? I suspect banks and finance companies would have turned him down had he approached them.

To his credit, Stan proposed a solution worth considering. He had some instruments and sound equipment he was willing to give up to cover the debt. I went over to his apartment to check out his wares and we struck a deal. I figured the chances were slim that I'd see any cash from him in the near future. May as well cut my losses, I thought. I ended up with a keyboard instrument and an electronic drum machine.

In spite of this setback, the rest of 1982 was full of enthusiastic activity. The income from the other loans allowed Susie and me to concentrate full time on our Scientology activities. I was also able to put a major portion of my time into my resurrected music career. We moved into a small house in Glendale, which was a fifteen-minute drive to the LA complex.

The house also had an unfinished downstairs that I turned into a music studio.

I was writing songs, recording demo tapes, and putting a band together, all the while getting lots of Scientology. It seemed like an ideal situation, and everything looked like it was going my way. Even after our six-month lease on the house was up, forcing us to move, fortune continued to work in my favor. The house next door was available for rent, and it was a little bit bigger, and not much more expensive. So we moved next door and life went on.

In November, I got a letter from one of my loan clients. He claimed that our loan agreement was illegal. He said according to someone he knew who had some legal knowledge, the amount of interest I was charging was against the law. He recommended that we redraw up the loan agreement.

I was shocked and confused. How could this have happened? Hadn't the Church been looking out for my interests? I got on the phone and talked to Kevin. He told me he'd looked into our loan deals and discovered there was indeed a legal issue. In fact, Kevin had already begun advising some of my loan clients to take this up with me so we could straighten it out. Kevin wasn't trying to screw me over. He was justifiably concerned that a bunch of Scientologists were engaged in illegal financial activities. I was concerned too. And I discovered that the Church wasn't going to be much help.

I went to see a lawyer that Kevin recommended who was a Scientologist. My consultation was brief and conclusive. I was in violation of usury laws, popularly known as "loan sharking." I was charging twenty percent interest, the rate that credit card companies were charging at the time. I wasn't an accredited financial organization, and needed a license to do what I was doing. It was unlikely I would qualify as a loan company even if I wanted to go through the process of certification. My lawyer recommended I just revise the loan agreements and set the interest at ten percent, the legal maximum for private-party loans.

I had no problem convincing my debtors to renegotiate. After all, the deal was working out in their favor. I was the one that was going to take a hit. By cutting the interest in half, all of the potency from my fly-by-night investment scheme was gone. I had to admit that I'd taken some foolish advice. But what could I do about it now?

I considered taking legal action, but the thought of suing the Church was much too intimidating. I knew they'd fight tooth and nail, expel me, and try to create a rift between Susie and me. Their official position would be that any restitution due to me would have to come from Darcy and Greg who put the shady deal together.

I knew the Church wouldn't vouch for them, much less accept any liability on their behalf. And even if I chose to take legal action against Darcy and Greg, I was still bound by policies regarding taking fellow Scientologists to court. Any solution I could think of conveniently worked out in the favor of the Church.

What outrageous irony! Any legal action I might take would have to go through the Church justice system. The ethics procedures which I thought were backing me up, were now protecting two Scientologists who had wrecked my income and put me at financial risk. And what could I collect from two poorly paid ex-Sea Org members? I had virtually no chance of recovering my losses anyway.

But I could get notoriety. By suing the Church, I might gain national public attention. Meanwhile, I'd be expelled, declared a *Suppressive Person*, and my Scientology friends would be forbidden to have anything to do with me. And I assumed that if I were to become an enemy of the Church, I'd be subject to aggressive scrutiny in an effort to damage my reputation. I didn't want that much drama suddenly thrust into my life.

In a practical sense, there was no one to blame but myself. Though I'd been misled and cheated from the day I sold my stock, it would be virtually impossible to get any compensation. I tried not to let it affect my overall relationship with Scientology. Somehow I would press on.

■ *IN RETROSPECT:* The reader might think that the loan disaster would have been the impetus that got me to leave the Church. I did consider it. But it was a potentially complicated solution with consequences I had to take into account. I concluded that no good would come of it.

I had no beef with Scientology as a subject, nor any argument with any of Hubbard's writings. And I was looking forward to getting auditing all the way through OT VII, and all of the auditor training I'd already paid for. So I managed to stay focused on the bigger picture: Get audited, get trained, help expand the Church, and be among the Scientologists who were actively improving conditions in society. ■

Chapter 11

Politics, Religion and Money

See Glossary for: *Squirrel*

In spite of my difficulties in the world of high finance, I was in good spirits in the summer of 1982. My wife, son, and I were living in a nice little house in Glendale, and I was enthusiastically building a music career. I teamed up with a fellow Scientologist, Walt, who used to work at the Westwood Mission with me. We formed a band based on our songwriting collaborations. I transformed the ground floor "basement" into a fortified oasis, sound-proofed with canvas and carpet remnants and filled with instruments and recording equipment. My studio was my very own kingdom, where music often emanated well into the night.

Just as important, my wife and I began our next phase of spiritual advancement—the OT levels. Now we were in the big time. We were about to enter the highest echelons of Scientology, occupied by a relatively elite few. There were your rank-and-file-Scientologists, and then there were your OTs who were often looked upon with awe and respect. Even in L.A., one of the most concentrated areas of Scientologists, where OT processing was delivered on a regular basis, the OT Scientologists were always singled out as the vanguard of the Scientology movement.

■ *IN RETROSPECT:* Are there any real OTs in Scientology? Scientologists claim there are. Over the years the

Church has compiled reams of anecdotal testimonies from Scientologists who claim to have experienced some sort of "OT phenomena." There are plenty of stories of clairvoyance, telepathy, and mind-over-matter phenomena. Advanced Scientologists believe they have the ability to cause things to happen, simply by determining it so.

On the other hand, critics like to point out that such claims have never stood the test of scientific scrutiny. And they like to point out that the public at large has never seen any Scientologists levitate, bend spoons with their minds, or make apparition-like appearances in some other-dimension-like form.

Personally, I've always been an enthusiast of "psychic phenomena," even before my encounter with Scientology. I happen to believe that paranormal, supernormal, and quasi-normal things occur everywhere from time to time. Scientologists like to claim it happens to them a lot, and there was a time I believed it was all true. Nowadays I think the superhuman abilities that Scientologists lay claim to tend to be hyped and overstated. ■

Susie and I continued on up the OT levels and all seemed well. However, behind the scenes, trouble was brewing within, affecting the highest ranks of Church management. Because of my connection with Westwood Mission, I was aware of some of the conflicts that were cropping up. What I didn't know was there was significant dissent coming from a number of Church leaders within the Mission network.

For many Scientologists, 1982 was the beginning of the end for the Church. The Church of Spiritual Technology was incorporated that year and given the rights to all of Hubbard's Dianetics and Scientology writings and lectures. That same year, the Church of Scientology International was overhauled and reincorporated. But the first real bombshell didn't hit until

July. Church executives at the highest levels were being removed from their posts.

Most Scientologists had little or no knowledge of the upheaval that was going on. It wasn't until a bulletin issued in August by Hubbard that Scientologists got any indication of the inner turmoil going on. David Mayo, the Church's Senior Case Supervisor, and considered the highest trained Scientologist in the Church was removed from his post and declared a Suppressive Person. This was devastating news. Not only had Mayo been regarded as the top auditor on the planet and one of the Church's most trusted members, he was also known as L. Ron Hubbard's personal auditor.

A political purge was in progress, and most Scientologists were unaware of the sweeping changes taking place. In October, the Church held a Mission Holder's conference in San Francisco, to brief executives on all of the organizational changes, especially those that would affect the Mission network. Attendees were informed that from here on out, the misapplication of Scientology and Dianetics would be viewed as a violation of trademarks. The Church's Religious Technology Center had been given complete legal authority to issue, restrict, and cancel Mission charters, as well as all Church related certifications. Mission Holders were told that they were now dealing with a tough and ruthless management team.

Management also announced an unprecedented and draconian policy that would eventually take a devastating toll on a number of Churches. A new administrative unit had been established, called the Finance Police, complete with a Finance Dictator at the top. For starters, Missions were required to give 5% of their weekly income to fund a new Dianetics campaign. Strict new policies were implemented restricting a Mission's ability to service their public and hold on to staff. Severe penalties for any violations were levied from $2,000 to $10,000 per violation. To insure compliance, all Missions were required to allow Finance Police verification teams to conduct inspections to ensure that Missions were falling in line with Church management. To this end, the Finance Police was authorized to charge Missions $15,000 per day for the privilege of being inspected.

As the Finance Police moved into action, they began charging Missions tens, even hundreds of thousands of dollars for their inspections. Missions were also forced to pay additional penalties for violations of the new policies. A lot of Scientologists were scratching their heads over this new harsh style of top-down management.

A number of Missions Holders did more than scratch their heads. Some quit in disgust, others tried to continue operating independently. Those who quit were expelled and declared Suppressive Persons. Those who tried to operate independently had their charters revoked and all of their certifications cancelled. They were then labeled "splinter groups" and charged with undermining the Church of Scientology. Lawsuits and litigation followed.

From 1981 through 1982, the Church of Scientology lost a significant number of their most successful and respected Mission Holders. Hundreds of dissident Church staff were expelled. Other execs were coming under scrutiny. The Church kept a watchful eye on dissenters, wary that disaffected Scientologists had the potential to become traitors and mutineers. Peter, the Westwood Mission Holder was one who had come under such scrutiny.

Peter had been an outspoken critic of management's treatment of the Mission network since 1980, but he usually knew when to back off. Though regarded by some Church execs as a loose cannon, Peter was respected, well liked, and was well connected within the Church. But in 1982 his contrary ways caught up with him.

A Committee of Evidence was called on Peter and his wife Lisa, alleging mismanagement of their Mission, misapplication of Scientology, and violations of official Church policy. An investigation ensued, and in February 1983, Scientology Missions International removed Peter as the Mission Holder of Westwood, and suspended all of his certifications, classifications and awards. Lisa's certs and classifications were summarily cancelled. Peter's Mission was literally taken away from him.

A whispering undercurrent of dissatisfaction and disagreement was seeping through the Church. Scientologists were leaving in noticeable numbers. Some staff left in protest, others were forced out by official edicts. Some even tried to establish their own independent Scientology organizations. In spite of this wave of disaffection, the Church managed to keep most of it under wraps. There were no official reports being released, and Scientologists had to rely on rumor grapevines for any news. Discussions regarding problems within the Church were discouraged and frowned upon. No one would openly talk about it.

I had my own problems. I was tangled up with my dozen or so Scientologists who I'd lent money to. Out of that group, I was having payment problems with half of them, and it was turning into a real headache. I was continuously calling them, cajoling them month after month to keep up with their monthly payments. I was dumfounded by their financial ineptness and lack of responsibility. These were supposedly reputable Scientologists, and it seemed to me that this should have been an Ethics issue that the Church would have wanted to deal with. But the ugly reality was that this was my problem. The Church was unwilling to get involved.

I was learning a rude lesson about Scientologists and their finances. Many had no qualms about putting their financial situation at risk along with anyone else's. I was dealing with people who would beg, borrow, and steal for the sake of getting their services paid for, and Church registrars were often encouraging this irresponsible approach.

Two cases in particular turned out to be especially troublesome. One of our debtors, Dan, had become dissatisfied with the Scientology services he was receiving. In protest, he stopped paying us. I was infuriated that a fellow Scientologist would stoop so low. In effect, he was holding our debt for ransom, insisting that the Church give him the sort of service he was demanding.

With the help of Kevin, the ASHO reg, I set up a Chaplain's Court. It's an informal arbitration used to settle minor disputes. The aggrieved parties make their case to a Church Minister overseeing the proceedings who then makes a recommendation.

Dan tried to make the case that because I loaned him the money for Church services, I shared some responsibility for the difficulties he was having with ASHO. I couldn't believe that a fellow Scientologist would have that kind of shameless temerity. Some fellow Scientologist this was!

The Minister simply pointed out that Dan had made an agreement with me, and was ethically and legally bound by it. Dan finally agreed to work something out. We drew up a new agreement, extending the loan and thereby decreasing the monthly payments.

Over time I came to realize that this sort of thing wasn't all that unusual. It was common practice for Scientologists to take on large debts through loans and credit cards, etc. The constant need for money to pay for services also persuaded many Scientologists into getting involved in get-rich-quick schemes. "Be your own boss" sort of businesses involving direct-mail or door-to-door selling was popular. And there was the multi-level marketing type of enterprise that had become the rage for many novice entrepreneurs.

I was led to believe that my loan scheme was different. It had been engineered by Church executives, and I had been assured that the Church would back me up at the first signs of difficulty. In reality, my scheme was just as hare-brained as anything else Scientologists got tangled up in. I may as well have been selling plastic combs, laser prints, gasoline additives, and the near infinite selection of health related products that so many "self-employed" Scientologists were touting.

One of my debtors proved to be more difficult than I thought could be possible. After several months of sporadic payments in partial amounts, Bruce stopped paying altogether and made himself scarce. I thought a lawsuit was in order, but that wasn't going to be easy. He was a Scientologist and was protected by the Church's system of Ethics. Initiating legal action with a fellow Scientologist was covered by Church policy, and I'd need official approval from the Church's International Justice Chief. Even so, such approval would only be granted after all other avenues of Church procedure had been pursued.

The Church of Scientology follows a well-established code of conduct practiced by police and military organizations, as well as the Vatican: You look out for your own by keeping misdeeds from public view, and administer justice from within. If I had any hope of getting my money, and remain a Church member in good standing, I was going to have to follow the Church's bureaucratic justice system.

After two letters to the IJC, it looked like I was getting the runaround. I received a letter from the Senior Director of Inspections and Reports International that brought up an aspect to my situation that had nothing to do with recovering my money. The Senior Director expressed a reluctance and unwillingness to approve legal action because of public relations considerations. The letter stated, "It actually would not be a good idea to drag this into the courtroom, due to the drawbacks this could have regarding Scientology."

It was a typical response. The irony of Scientology Ethics was rearing its head once again. The system I had put my faith in, that system I was so confident would back me up through thick and thin, was now standing in the way of my efforts of achieving justice. But as a Scientologist, I had no other choice than to put the wheels in motion and hope for the best.

My first step was to call a Chaplain's Court as I'd done previously with Dan. Neither I nor the Chaplain were surprised when Bruce didn't show up. From the beginning, he showed no signs of cooperation. I figured now I'd be able file a lawsuit. Not so. In a letter from the Deputy International Justice Chief, I was instructed to call a civil Committee of Evidence. It was more severe than a Chaplain's Court and fell under the jurisdiction of the Church's Ethics Division. Should Bruce refuse to comply, that would be grounds for expulsion. Once expelled, Bruce would no longer have the protection of the Church, and I would be free to take whatever legal action I wanted.

As the bureaucratic machinery rolled on, I was getting a grim lesson in Church sanctioned justice. I alone would suffer the consequences of any mishaps involving other

Scientologists. That lesson hit me one day like a ton of bricks when I came home to find an IRS agent sitting with my wife at the kitchen table. Though I was momentarily surprised, the visit wasn't totally unexpected. We owed a big chunk of capital gains taxes as a result of our sale of Seagate stock. Back when I was selling my stock and doling out loans, no one thought to mention the tax liabilities of my financial venture.

Susie and I spent about a half an hour with the IRS man working out a payment plan. It was manageable, and we eventually got the tax bill paid, no thanks to anyone in the Church. Meanwhile many of our remaining debtors continued to give us trouble. In the end, we came out big losers money-wise, when you factor in the taxes, lowered interest, delinquent payments, and outright defaults. Even the original sale of our Seagate stock was poorly engineered. Following the inept advice of Church executives had become an enormously expensive proposition.

■ IN RETROSPECT: The Church of Scientology was the primary reason for our financial debacle, yet Susie and I remained loyal members. I'm not sure if I can adequately explain why. We were both OT V by then, and we valued our auditing and training. It was something we didn't calculate in monetary terms. Susie and I wrote off the whole incident as a live and learn experience.

I can only speculate as to why we continued to stay with the Church. Perhaps we had entered into a kind of abusive relationship, the kind that battered women seem to have difficulty ending. Maybe like an abused wife, we'd become dysfunctionally dependent on the Church to the point that we'd convinced ourselves that the abuse wasn't all that bad. And just like the abused wife, maybe we also convinced ourselves that the Church of Scientology would reform its abusive ways.

There's one thing I can point to with a little more certainty: I was susceptible to Church intimidation. The prospect of being expelled from Scientology was an effective threat, similar I suspect to the Christian concept of eternal damnation. If I were to fall out of line with my Church, I believed that my spiritual future would have been put to an end forever. I was convinced that the Church of Scientology was so powerful that they had the means of somehow determining my fate for eternity. The Church itself truly believes this, and perhaps more important, most Scientologists believe it as well. ▩

In spite of our endless troubles with the Church, Susie and I continued to muddle through. In the Fall of 1983, Susie went to Flag to do the recently released OT VI and VII. I was going to the Advanced Organization, finishing up on OT V, and doing the OT Doctorate Course, which was based on a number of lectures Hubbard gave in Philadelphia in 1952.

▩ **BACKGROUND:** OT level auditing follows the basic principles Hubbard established in Dianetics. But there's one big difference. OT auditing addresses traumatic incidents that supposedly occurred millions of years ago. The "thetan" has carried this spiritual baggage for all of these years and has suffered ever since. Once relieved of these traumas, the individual regains abilities and powers that have been long lost and long forgotten. ▩

Meanwhile, the Church continued to have their troubles. It was a turbulent time, even though most Scientologists were unaware that problems existed. Prominent Scientologists continued to leave the Church to start their own groups. Former Senior Case Supervisor David Mayo started his own Scientology counseling group shortly after he was expelled.

Other ex-members followed suit, and began running their own practices. In spite of the Church's attempts to keep the disaffections under wraps, it was difficult not to notice there was an exodus in progress. One such Scientologist was my songwriting partner Walt.

I was aware of Walt's strained relationship with the Church, since we talked about it occasionally. He was still technically a staff member at Westwood Mission on some quasi-leave-of-absence. He didn't want to go back and I couldn't blame him. Since Peter's departure, there was no improvement there. But Walt expressed an antagonism towards Church management that I couldn't accept. Walt believed that the reorganizations taking place were ill advised and detrimental to Scientology. I had faith that things would eventually work themselves out.

Walt sometimes danced around the subject of possibly doing his OT levels outside of the Church. In Scientology parlance, that meant joining a *squirrel* group, something the Church didn't tolerate. We both knew such a move would get him expelled. One night he made a dire confession. He'd been studying OT materials with a splinter group and getting "outside" auditing. I could tell that Walt had made up his mind, so I didn't try to talk him out of it.

We both knew what the ramifications were. I'd be duty bound to report this to Church authorities, and sooner or later I'd be compelled to disconnect from him. It would be the end of our relationship. Walt understood and didn't seem to hold it against me. He knew that if I wanted to remain a Scientologist in good standing, I had no other choice.

We dissolved our musical partnership, and divvied up the instruments and recording equipment. My uneventful musical career seemed to be coming to an inconsequential end, as was my friendship with Walt. Perhaps I should have viewed the breakup as a sad loss, but that's not the way I felt. I was a still a loyal Scientologist, and I believed that what Walt had done was nothing short of joining up with the enemy. Without an ounce of regret, I ended all contact with him.

Chapter 12

The Church Marches On

See Glossary for: *PTS*

In 1984 my music career dwindled to near nonexistence. Walt took the recording equipment, and I got the Moog synthesizer. Our divorce settlement was complete. Loan payments trickled in. Susie was working part time, and it was time for me to start looking for a real job.

By this time, the old Guardian's Office had been replaced by the Office of Special Affairs. It was a PR makeover caused by the FBI raids in 1977. The court trial that followed exposed years of deceptive and insidious tactics the GO used to defend the Church. Eleven execs eventually went to jail. The formation of the Office of Special Affairs was meant to demonstrate that the Church had changed its ways.

The name changed but their function remained the same. OSA was now the Church's official legal and public relations arm. They were still understaffed, and depended on volunteers to help carry out many of their projects. Susie and I were ideal recruits. We were both OTs and therefore mentally and spiritually stable enough to bear up under the potentially upsetting information in which OSA was immersed.

Susie and I were qualified in another important area: We were already privy to the confidential upper level OT materials. This was crucial. Disaffected Scientologists were distributing OT III material, from memory or from stolen copies, and it put the Church into a state of near hysteria. OSA got itself wrapped up in a desperate attempt to prevent further exposure of the Church's most secret scriptures.

One source of their anxiety was a local paper called the *LA Weekly*. Ex-Scientologists were inserting OT III references into the *Weekly's* free personal ads. Susie joined a small brigade of Scientologists who would regularly glean through the *LA Weekly* personal ads, looking for OT III references. When something was found, they'd scour the streets looking for *Weekly* news bins. When they found one, they'd remove all the papers from it.

It was comedic how fixated the Church had become in their obsession to squelch the publishing of their confidential material. The anonymous pranksters must have thought the Church's mad caper hilarious. Even OSA eventually realized the futility of their task. Regularly removing every issue of a citywide publication was like pushing the tide back with a broom. And in the process, the Church was drawing attention to itself, creating a public curiosity towards the confidential material that they were trying to censor.

While all of this was going on, I was assisting OSA in a more modest fashion. Paula, the Westwood staffer who'd been kidnapped by her father, had filed a lawsuit against her deprogrammer. For several weeks I went through reams of court records and wrote summaries of the court case testimonies. It was tedious work, but I carried it out dutifully.

My next assignment was going to be a lot different than my mundane paralegal assistance. This new operation was a CIA-James Bond-Mission Impossible sort of plan. My mission, should I decide to accept it, would be to go to Santa Barbara, and infiltrate David Mayo's Advanced Ability Center. I was given two instructions. First, meet as many people as I could, and observe all that went on. The second assignment was more daunting as it required subterfuge and deceit. I was instructed to submit to an E-meter interview, then sign up for a course. Then I was supposed to write a check for the course and say I'd return in a week to start. Once the check was written, I'd call my bank and stop payment on the check. This super-spy plan was meant to disrupt Mayo's splinter group, and at the same time keep OSA abreast of their activities. It sounded like fun.

While getting briefed by my OSA contact, I was told that my debtor-in-default, Bruce R. was supposedly an active member of the Advanced Ability Center. How did OSA know about him? I'd never mentioned it, but it likely figured prominently in my Ethics folder. In OSA-styled due diligence, they must have reviewed my "dossier" before enlisting me.

I accepted my role of agent provocateur with enthusiastic relish. It was better than being Batman. Accompanying me behind enemy lines was an ex-GO staff member who was now a public Scientologist. I thought it was cool that I'd be working with a veteran of Church counter-intelligence operations who'd be showing me the ropes.

When we arrived in Santa Barbara, Dave said the first thing we needed to do was "look around and get a lay of the land." Wow, just like being in the Green Berets. This was going to be great.

The Advanced Ability Center operated in a residential house in a nice suburban Santa Barbara neighborhood. It was Saturday, the day when the ACC held informal gatherings— sort of an open-house affair for new public. Posing as new public, Dave and I split up to create whatever mischief an opportunity might present.

I got a tour of the house, met a few staff and finally sat down with a registrar. He was a personable guy, a little bit younger than me. I told him I'd become dissatisfied with the Church, especially the high prices, but wanted to continue my auditing and training. He said my situation wasn't all that unique, that a lot of people like me were leaving the Church.

Everyone there seemed real nice, and I wondered how such a nice guy could have turned against the Church. I reasoned that I was dealing with misled dupes, led astray by the insidious forces designed to topple Scientology.

My next step was to get an interview on the E-meter with their Director of Processing. That was Julie Mayo, the newlywed wife of David Mayo and also his former assistant while they were still in the Church.

I'd received some basic instructions and drilling from OSA and I felt well prepared. I don't recall the specific questions, but they seemed innocuous enough. Then she asked me, "Are you *PTS* to the Church?" That was my cue to let out a regretful sigh, look at the floor and ponder for a moment. Then I looked up as if I just had some realization and said as sincere as I could, "Yeah, I think I am."

In Scientology, people who were PTS (Potential Trouble Source) are considered to be that way because of some connection to a Suppressive Person or Group. Supposedly, a PTS person will get sick frequently and get into all kinds of personal trouble. By saying I was PTS to the Church, I had implied that I believed the Church was suppressing me. That's what Julie was looking for.

I was in. Next stop, the Registrar's Office. The reg recommended that I sign up for some auditing designed to repair the damage that the Church had caused me. The amount wasn't very much by orthodox Church of Scientology standards—just a few hundred dollars. I whipped out my check book, signed up for the auditing, and said I'd be back the following weekend to do my service.

Having gained their confidence, it was time for some reconnaissance work. This secret agent stuff was turning out to be pretty easy. The backyard barbecue was in full swing, and I mingled, keeping my eyes and ears open for anything that might be worth reporting back to OSA. I saw a fairly young guy standing in the corner by himself, eating a hamburger. I walked up to him and started a conversation. He boasted he was the son of Heber Jentzsch*, the man who used to head up the old Guardians Office. I think I was supposed to be impressed by the irony in that, but I just played it cool and nodded.

*I didn't know much about Heber's family history, but I took the guy at his word. If what he said was true, it could only have been Peter Gillham Jr., son of Heber's former wife, Yvonne. Perhaps there are some old-timers out there that can confirm this.

As I continued to wander through the crowd, I saw David Mayo speaking with some guests. I recognized him as I'd seen his picture in Scientology magazines. He'd also appeared in a Church produced film titled, The Secret of Flag Results, which was a promotional flick for the Flag Land Base. On film, Mayo was less than charismatic, just the opposite of L. Ron Hubbard. My impression of Mayo, based on the film, was that he was a low key sort of guy without much of a dynamic personality. Seeing him in person confirmed that impression.

Though he was conservative in appearance and demeanor, it didn't deter me from making an overt and gregarious overture. I walked up to the group with whom he was talking, stood there and smiled expectantly like a fan seeking an autograph. I was impossible to ignore. He stopped talking, looked at me, and I jumped in, held out my hand and said,

"You're David Mayo. Hi, I'm Chris Shugart." His expression didn't change much as he asked, "Is there something I can do for you?" I continued with my eager admirer routine and said, "I just wanted to meet you and say 'hi.'" He barely smiled, nodded, but said nothing. I guess I didn't create much of an impression. Under the circumstances, I suppose that was a good thing. The conversation pretty much ended there.

On the ride home, I had an eye-opening conversation with Dave, my partner in crime. I brought up my situation with Bruce R., and Dave said matter-of-factly, "He's an intelligence agent who works for the Air Force." How did he know that, I asked?

Dave then related an unbelievable and slightly disturbing story. He told me that when he was in the Guardians Office, the Church had become suspicious of Bruce. Dave said he posed as his gay lover and actually lived with him briefly in order to gather more information. I wasn't eager for more details. It was all I could do to digest the little information I'd just gotten and it was making my head swim.

What had I gotten myself into? What was the Church of Scientology's real strategy here? The Church seemed willing to go through elaborate subterfuge to deal with Bruce R., yet when I tried to initiate a sound and justifiable lawsuit against him, I was getting the runaround. My shock turned into confusion.

I felt like I was looking at a jigsaw puzzle with a lot of pieces missing, and I had no idea what to make of it. It occurred to me that I may have stumbled onto something much bigger than I was prepared to deal with. Intuitively, I sensed that it might be best for me to back off. I felt like I was on the verge of "knowing too much" as if I were about to become some unsuspecting victim in a spy novel. I dropped the matter and never inquired further to anyone in the Church. As Ray Davies said, "When in doubt, trust your paranoia."

■ **IN RETROSPECT:** Years later I discovered some corroboration of this unbelievable story. I came across a video of Mike McClaughry who was a former intelligence operative for the Guardians Office. According to McClaughry, Bruce R. was a captain in U.S. Air Force intelligence who was on lines at ASHO and was trying to infiltrate the Church in an attempt to steal confidential documents pertaining to the OT levels. I still don't know what to think. ■

Back at headquarters, at the Advanced Org, I gave my OSA contact a complete debriefing. The lady I reported to was young, friendly, and upbeat—not the type you'd expect to be associated with espionage and intrigue.

As I related details, my contact seemed like she was after something in particular. The conversation kept returning back to David Mayo. How did he look? Did he look healthy? Did he look ill? It was like OSA had already come to their own conclusions about Mayo and wanted me to merely confirm what they already suspected. In any case, the mission was accomplished, though I wasn't sure what exactly had been accomplished.

There's an epilogue to this caper that happened a couple of weeks later. OSA wasn't ready to close the case quite yet. They were aware of my defaulted loan with Bruce R. Although they weren't so concerned with the money he owed me, they had a plan they thought could benefit both OSA and me. They convinced me to go back to Santa Barbara, and complain to the organization that one of their members was trying to rip me off. The thinking was that if I made this fact known to the ACC, it would somehow upset their ranks. It was a fool's errand, but by now I'd become a loyal agent of OSA, and I didn't have the nerve to turn them down. I may as well finish what I started.

My second trip to Santa Barbara ended with a predictable result. I met with the ACC Executive Director and brought up the loan issue, but it was to no avail. He practically threw me out of his office. My disagreements with Bruce were neither his concern nor the ACC's. He simply suggested I take up the matter with Bruce.

I thought that this was going to be the end of the whole affair, but it wasn't. When it comes to battling their enemies, Scientologists can be tenacious as badgers. My OSA contact suggested I ought to go to the police and file an official report accusing Bruce R. of criminal fraud. I was convinced that this was nothing but an idiotic stunt headed for failure. Although my heart wasn't in it anymore, I played along. I figured if I went through the motions of this feeble plan, I'd be done with it for good.

I showed up one afternoon at the Northwest Precinct of the Los Angeles Police Department with a handful of documents. I told the Desk Officer I wanted to speak to a detective to report a fraudulent crime. Moments later I was speaking to a detective and showing him the incriminating evidence. He gave me a kindly smile, the sort of look you might have when you need to humor a lunatic. He told me he thought my best option was to consult a lawyer. He wasn't even willing to file a report. I couldn't blame him. I felt a little ridiculous, and was glad to get out of there.

They say that the wheels of justice can turn slowly. That goes double for Scientology justice. After two years of this Scientology Ethics theater-of-the-absurd, I finally received an approval to sue Bruce R. I didn't even get anything formal in writing. All I received was a dispassionate and very brief telex that wasn't even sent to me, but rather sent to ASHO. All it said was:

RE: BRUCE R:
YES HE IS CONFIRMED W MAYO. SHUGART WILL NOW SUE IF NECESSARY

Two years of bureaucratic runaround, and this is all I got out of it. It was a ridiculous punctuation mark put at the end of a lengthy and ridiculous affair.

I finally consulted a lawyer. Big deal. The lawyer recommended that I drop the matter. In his estimation, I had almost no chance of collecting any money, even if I were to get a favorable judgment. So much time had gone by that I would have a hard time attaching, much less finding any of Bruce's assets. My lawyer predicted that in a final dodge, Bruce would declare bankruptcy and just laugh about the whole thing. He was probably already laughing.

■ ***IN RETROSPECT:*** I've since re-examined everything I'd learned about the Bruce R. affair. I organized a time line that shows that there must have been at least a few people within the Church that knew who Bruce really was. In fact, it's possible that he had already become a known malcontent by the time I loaned him the money.

Most likely, I'd been a pawn in a nonsensical chess game that could only rival Lewis Carroll's *Through the Looking Glass*. The Church was guilty of incompetence at best, outright malfeasance at worst. Either way, I was the one who lost the game.

I can only speculate why I couldn't get any cooperation from the Church. My best guess is that the Church wanted to nail Bruce R. as a big time infiltrator, and they didn't want me tangling up their efforts with a lawsuit. In the grand scheme of Church affairs, my situation was low priority.

In spite of all that had happened, I remained steadfast in my loyalty to the Church. Again, the question must be asked: Why? Is there a sensible explanation?

Perhaps the best way to understand my thinking at the time would be to put it in the context of war. As a Scientologist, I often felt like a soldier in a large army fighting an enemy of government interlopers, a biased press with hostile agendas, and an insidious psychiatric industry, all bent on molding mankind to their own selfish and destructive ends. L. Ron Hubbard's antagonism towards these institutions crops up many times in his writings.

Here I was engaged in battle, fighting the good fight, for God, country and Scientology. I believed in the cause and I trusted the leadership. In war there are casualties, and sometimes they come not at the hand of the enemy, but by friendly fire. And casualties can sometimes come from flawed plans or ill-conceived tactics.

Hubbard has played on this metaphor more than a few times. In Ron's *Journal 34* Hubbard states,

"Oh, yes, we've had some casualties . . . But that is the way with wars: not only combatants but innocent bystanders can get wounded." [2]

I understood this deeply. There were inherent risks in being a dedicated Scientologist. Such were the fortunes of war. ■

Other than my recent drama, I was otherwise leading a pretty normal life. After being laid off from a North Hollywood ad agency, I found a job in downtown L.A. in the advertising department of a large cosmetics manufacturer and distributor.

It was 1985 and Susie was pregnant with our second child. On week nights I was at ASHO doing auditor training. My life had subsided to a comfortable routine—that is until this one particular evening...

It was about 9:15 PM when someone came into the course room and handed the supervisor a note. The course sup interrupted our study with an unprecedented announcement. "That's it. Let me have your attention. We've been instructed to report to Lebanon Hall for an important briefing." In all of my years in Scientology, course study had never been interrupted for anything. Whatever it was, this had to be big. It looked like life was going to get more interesting.

Lebanon Hall was a small auditorium, part of the LA complex used to put on events, meetings, and sometimes Sunday services. The place was filled to the max, packed with students from ASHO, LA Org, and the Advanced Org. Everyone had been pulled off their courses to attend this briefing. The Church was always embroiled in some kind of controversy. Still, I didn't know what this was going to be about.

Ken Hoden, President of the L.A. Chapter of the Church of Scientology took the stage and began his speech. "As many of you know, there's been a lawsuit pending in Portland surrounding the Julie Christofferson case."

I was vaguely aware of the lawsuit. In 1977, Christofferson had taken the Church to court in an attempt to get a $3,000 refund. She'd received a $2.1 million award in 1979 that was overturned in 1982. There was still legal action going on, and the stakes were getting high. But I had no idea how high they'd become. Hoden continued, "The Portland Judge Donald Londer has awarded Julie Christofferson thirty-nine million dollars."

Holy cow! The Church always wins its court cases, I thought. How did this happen? What are we going to do now? I'm sure most Scientologists in the auditorium were as shocked as I was. Curiously, Hoden looked upbeat, even amused by the bombshell he'd just dropped. "You know what we're going to do?" he asked. "We're going to Portland! And we're leaving tonight!" He pointed towards the door as if he were leading the way. The crowd cheered.

Though my mind was reeling with what this might mean for Scientology, I understood there was something important unfolding before my eyes. This was an all-hands call to arms unprecedented in Scientology history. It was time to go on the attack. Retreat was not an option. Win or die in the attempt.

Outside of Lebanon Hall, transportation was already being arranged for the long trip. A number of buses were gearing up and getting ready to roll. We'd be leaving in a matter of hours.

My old Scientologist friend Skip, who first suggested that I do a Scientology course, found me in the crowd that was developing outside the complex. He shouted, "Hey Chris, you wanna drive up with us?" Sounded good to me. I wasn't looking forward to a twelve hour bus ride. Skip was organizing a two car convoy and eight passengers to make the long drive to Portland. There'd be Skip and me, a couple of ASHO students, and some others from LA Org who would make up our impromptu platoon. We all agreed we'd meet back at the complex in an hour or so, enough time to pack whatever it was we thought we were going to need.

On my drive home I had a few moments of quiet reflection, which gave me a chance to assess the situation. I was somewhat of a protest veteran from my previous experiences marching for Church causes. I figured the Church would stage a well organized protest in Portland similar to what I'd experienced in L.A., only a lot bigger.

For the first time, Church executives had given the go-ahead to pull students off their courses. There'd never been anything remotely like this before. Surely this was our most desperate hour.

I got home and briefed Susie on what I'd learned. Then I said, "The Church needs people to go up to Portland to get the judge to overturn the judgment. I have to do this." Susie understood the gravity of the situation. But she did caution me that if things got out of hand in Portland, I needed to keep in mind I might get thrown in jail. It was an outside possibility, but that kind of overt sixties-style civil disobedience wasn't the Church's style.

I had a concern much closer to home. Susie was four months pregnant and I had some misgivings about leaving her alone to manage the household while I was gone. But the biggest risk I'd be taking was how this was going to affect my job position. I'd been working at my new downtown job for only six weeks, and now I was going to take some "emergency" time off. In wartime, you're sometimes compelled to accept extraordinary risks above and beyond the call of duty. Such was the case now.

I hadn't a clue how long I'd be gone and no idea where I'd be sleeping. I figured my best bet was to travel as light as possible. I felt like some Special Forces commando gearing up for a raid. I had a small backpack with a change of clothes, a heavy jacket, and a rolled up blanket tethered with rope. I also brought a canteen, a Swiss Army knife, a flashlight, some string, some wire, a book of matches, and a street map of Portland I'd torn out of an old Auto Club atlas. It probably wasn't exactly the sort of thing they issued you in the Army Rangers, but I'd done a fair amount of camping in my time and I felt pretty well prepared for whatever was in store.

I told Susie to call my work on Monday and tell them I'd be gone for a couple of days to handle a personal emergency. For family and non-Scientologist friends, our cover story was that I was on a business trip. As I was about to leave, I told Susie I'd call as soon as I could. We both felt as if I were boarding a troop transport headed for the front. "Take care of yourself," she said.

I got back to the Complex a little after 11 PM. The street was full of activity as Scientologists were getting organized for the long trip. It made me think of soldiers preparing for the D-Day Normandy landing. The rest of my crew hadn't yet showed, so I wandered around hoping I might get a better idea of what I was getting myself into.

When I met up with my traveling entourage I got a little ribbing about my Rambo-esque gear and accessories. The kidding ended when one of the drivers started fretting about the front license plate on his car which was hanging precariously by one screw, looking like it was about to fall off. I knelt down, pulled out my wire and had the plate lashed securely in moments. Everyone called me Commando after that.

It was well after midnight by the time we actually hit the road. Now we were off to Portland, eight Scientologists in two cars—an old Volkswagen station wagon and a Honda hatchback. Not exactly first class, but better than riding in an old school bus. We drove through the night, and all the next day. By late Saturday afternoon, we were in Weed, just south of Lake Shasta. We'd stopped for gas and I took the opportunity to call home. All I got was our answering machine, so I left a message. I learned later in a subsequent phone call that Susie had been pressed into service on the home front, making phone calls and coordinating logistics. Other Scientologists in L.A. were being similarly deployed.

124

The course rooms were almost empty now, and it created a serious and unusual problem the Church never had to deal with before. The orgs' production stats were crashing due to the lack of activity. The Church found itself fighting on two fronts, trying to get thousands of Scientologists to Portland, but at the same time keep the Churches operating at their normal level of activity.

Finally, our two-car mobile assault unit got into Portland that Saturday night around 10:30 PM. Our rendezvous point was supposed to be the Portland Scientology Mission. We decided to split up and look for good places to park overnight. I volunteered to park one of the cars and said I'd catch up with everyone later. We all agreed that for now it was every man for himself until Sunday when we'd regroup.

The "Battle of Portland" was about to begin.

Chapter 13

A Modern Day Crusade

It was close to midnight by the time I walked into the Portland Mission. The place was wall-to-wall people and buzzing like a beehive. There was no way of telling if anyone was in charge. For all I knew, maybe nobody was. I wandered around, squeezing my way through the mass of bodies. Everyone must have had the same question I had: "OK, I'm here, now what?"

I figured the best thing to do was to relax and wait. I found an empty room that looked like it must have been one of the course rooms. I crawled under a table and thought I might try to get some sleep. No telling how many opportunities like this I might get. A few others followed my lead and started staking out floor space. We might be bunking here for the night. In an hour I was drifting off to sleep, when the door opened, the light turned on and a voice announced "That's it. We're transporting everyone to the Org. Let's get this place cleaned up."

Well, finally someone in charge.

It was a five minute drive to the Portland Class IV Church, and we arrived there around 2:00 AM. Sea Org members were being berthed elsewhere and I was on my own to find a place to sleep. What looked like the main course room was covered with people on the floor already asleep. I fumbled my way through the dark and laid down on my blanket on the hard wood floor, my backpack for a pillow, and my jacket for a blanket. I managed to get a few hours of sleep.

In the morning, Scientologists were guided onto buses and taken to the big park downtown, right in front of the Portland courthouse. Hundreds of demonstrators had already arrived, and many more were expected. A stage was under construction and protest signs were being made.

One lady was looking for volunteers who could sing. That was definitely my department. The lady was the director of a Scientology choir that performed frequently in L.A. She and some of her singers had come to Portland and were now in the process of putting together a few songs for the big rally that was evolving before our eyes. She handed me some sheet music and said they'd be rehearsing shortly.

The park was starting to take on the look of an organized activity. The stage was finished, complete with a sound system. A large banner spanned the entire structure that read "Religious Freedom Crusade." The event was under way.

The PA system was fired up and a man stepped up to the microphone and announced, "This is happening." The speaker was Jeff Pommerantz who would continue to be the master of ceremonies throughout the demonstration events. Jeff was a bit-part actor that no one had ever heard of, but he made a name for himself in Portland that would last for years. He became sort of an all-purpose master of ceremonies for many subsequent Church rallies and events.

Our thrown together choir was the first entertainment segment of the event. We opened with *God Bless America*, then went straight into the heavyweight material. Our rendition of Handel's *Hallelujah Chorale* was a bit ragged, but our closing number, the generically Christian *Let Peace Begin With Me* went well.

The rest of the day was a series of speeches interspliced with musical entertainment. A few local talents comprised of Portland Scientologists performed, as did a couple of performers from L.A. The demonstration was being promoted as an international event, so one of the big highlights was going to be the arrival of a group of protestors all the way from Italy. They arrived late in the day, a half dozen Italian Scientologists driving a white van with a large Italian flag proudly flapping outside the window. They circled the park a couple of times, honking their horn as the crowd cheered.

To cap off the event, we staged a candlelight vigil in the name of religious freedom, thus ending Day One of the Portland Religious Freedom Crusade. The solidarity was infectious and inspiring, and in spite of whatever difficulties that might lie ahead, morale was high. Sunday had come and gone, and Monday would be a new day of events.

A lot of the demonstrators were bunking in a gymnasium that belonged to a school run by Scientologists. That sounded like a grim prospect. As luck would have it, one lady in our group had a younger brother who lived not very far from downtown Portland. She'd already cleared it with him, and we'd be spending the night at his house. That was fabulously good news.

On Monday, everyone was instructed to gather at the courthouse early in the morning. Protest signs were issued and we started marching around the building. We wanted to make sure that people driving to work would see the spectacle. For several hours, hundreds of Scientologists marched around and around the courthouse. I lost count of how many times we sang *We Shall Overcome.*

Day Two looked like it was turning into a success. The media was taking notice. We were on the front page of the local papers, and also on TV news across the country. All the while, Church PR made a conscious effort to portray us as the good guys fighting injustice.

If nothing else, our protest demonstration was evidence of how well organized the Church can be on the fly. There was one factor however, that hadn't been adequately addressed: money. There was the cost of transportation, cost of materials, and the cost of housing the dozens of Church staff running the demonstration. The Church was even providing food for hundreds of Scientologists who may have arrived in Portland with little or no money. Behind the scenes, expenses were piling up.

Some Sea Org officer came up to me, seemingly out of nowhere, took me aside and explained that the Religious Freedom Crusade was in immediate need of cash to keep the event afloat. She told me that they were in the process of putting together something called the Crusade Org which from now on would be the official organization surrounding the entire activity. She asked me if I would go through the crowd and solicit donations. There was such a can-do spirit running through the whole event that I didn't need to think twice about accepting.

I was given a plastic container, and I started making the rounds, uninhibited in a way that was out of character for me. I quickly devised a sales pitch and spoke to dozens of Scientologists, telling them that we needed money to keep the event going. I collected about $250 in less than fifteen minutes.

The girl who had recruited me was impressed with my instant success. She wanted to take me to their headquarters, turn in the money, and then have me write up a description of whatever it was I did that would account for my success. This is common practice within Scientology organizations. If someone is successful at something, you find out what it was they did, and to the degree that you can duplicate the successful action, you should be able to duplicate the result. So I wrote up my successful actions, which would presumably become the template for other Scientologist volunteers. They would in turn, circulate through the crowd and solicit for more funds.

I was escorted to what I guessed was a Church command post—a small hotel room in an old hotel just on the outskirts of downtown. There was some Church exec on the phone in the middle of some heated negotiation. I could tell from his end of the conversation that he was talking to some hotel personnel regarding an outstanding bill. As best as I could gather, the Church was running up a large phone bill and the hotel was asking for money and threatening to cut off the phone service. I listened to the Church exec, as he promised profusely that he had money in hand to pay the bill. I must have arrived just in time.

Once off the phone, the exec explained to me that Church management was unwilling to indiscriminately disburse money from their treasury. You couldn't just set up some new operation and automatically expect to receive funding. There was policy and procedure that had to be followed. What Church division should the money come from? From the Western Continental Church? From Church of Scientology International? There was red tape involved.

I suppose that strictly speaking, the Religious Freedom Crusade was under the auspices of the Office of Special Affairs. My guess was that OSA wasn't well funded to begin with and now they were strapped for cash. The solution? Form a new organization, call it the Crusade Org, and get it funded by Church parishioners. This in fact was exactly what was occurring right before my eyes.

By the evening, the Portland rally had moved to a larger park along the Willamette River. The whole thing was starting to take on the look of a big outdoor rock festival. The music entertainment continued, mostly by no-names and big-time wannabees. However that would change by the following evening. John Travolta and Chick Corea, two of the Church's most prominent celebrities, were scheduled to make an appearance.

Now it was decision time for our eight-person entourage. How long were we staying? It was a mixed consensus. A few wanted to stay, if for no other reason than to see Travolta and Corea. Skip's wife was on staff at L.A. Org and really needed to get back. So did I. I didn't want to put undue strain on my relationship with my relatively new employer. She and I decided that we would fly back to L.A. on Tuesday.

Although my life settled down quickly, the Portland Crusade continued for two more weeks. I even considered returning there during the Memorial Day weekend. For those two weeks, Portland became the cause celèbre for Scientologists around the world. Portland had become a battle cry like "remember the Alamo." If you were a Scientologist, you were expected to be on course or in an auditing session, or you were expected to be marching in Portland. At the very least you were expected to be donating money to the Crusade Org and volunteering your time helping maintain logistics.

On the eve when the Portland judge Donald Londer was to make the jury decision official, there was an all-night vigil in front of the Portland court house. As a gesture of solidarity, there was a similar vigil being staged at the L.A. complex. I was there all night and managed to get through the next work day without any sleep.

The Church had hoped that the Portland demonstrations would compel Judge Londer to reconsider his verdict and perhaps even get him to declare a mistrial. Through all of the drama, the day of the judge's decision turned out to be anti-climactic. Londer showed up that morning and decided to delay indefinitely his final decision on the case. Still, it was a minor victory at least. Moreover, it was a good example of how Scientology approaches the legal process. If you can't win, try to drag out the case in an endless maze of legal moves designed to pound your opponent into a bureaucratic stupor.

Two months later, the Church finally triumphed when Judge Londer declared a mistrial based on some legal technicalities. This was a huge victory for Scientologists. But in spite of this good fortune, the Church was soon to get embroiled in more legal entanglements.

Like most Scientologists, I was mostly unaware of what was going on within the Church's legal affairs. Every now and then you might here about some lawsuit, but they always seemed to come and go. The Church hardly ever released details to the Scientology public. Only when they scored a big victory, as in the Christofferson case, would the Church make a public announcement. And only when they felt immediately threatened did they bring Scientologists into the loop. Such was the case involving former Scientologist Larry Wollersheim.

In November 1985, Susie and I were busy with our newborn girl, only days old. We hardly had time for Church activism. But Scientologists were on the warpath once again in an attempt to prevent the confidential OT III materials from being entered into court records from the Wollersheim case. I received a phone call one evening from someone representing the now officially established Crusade Org. He sounded young, confident, and energetic as he laid out the current court situation. He instructed me, with a presumptuous air of authority, that I needed to appear at the L.A. courthouse the next morning.

I told him that I couldn't make it. I had a new baby, just a week old, and my wife was still convalescing. Perfectly prudent and reasonable, I thought. The caller didn't seem to think so. It was as if he didn't hear me. His response was audacious and a little arrogant. "Do you understand the gravity of what I'm saying," he asked. "We're talking about confidential materials being released to the public." I was annoyed and insulted by his callous disregard for my situation. I curtly declined.

■ IN RETROSPECT: Indifferent lack of concern for the personal lives of individual Scientologists is a prevalent attitude within the Church organization. Group goals are usually senior to individual needs. Scientologists accept the fact that the individual may occasionally suffer for the greater good of the Church. It's Machiavellian to be sure, but it's also Hubbard's policy. Scientologists are convinced that their ends always justify their means. I marvel now at the amount of abuse Scientologists are willing to tolerate for the "good of the Church." ■

The Wollersheim case was a tricky situation. The materials of OT III were the most intensely guarded secrets in Scientology. I believed, like most Scientologists, that this would be an unprecedented revelation with catastrophic consequences should the confidential materials become accessible to the public.

The Church is extremely strict on its own members in this area. I got into trouble once for leaving my auditing room unattended for a moment to get a drink of water. I didn't even have any of Hubbard's confidential writings, just my own handwritten auditing reports which were nothing but a chronological record of the OT processes I had run. That infraction alone earned me a trip to the Ethics Officer. I had to complete an Ethics program before I could resume my auditing.

Some Scientologists have addressed this security issue by carrying their auditing materials in a briefcase handcuffed to their wrists by a short chain. It always looked like something out of a James Bond movie to me.

■ *IN RETROSPECT:* I occasionally thought that perhaps the Church's tight security was a little over the top. It's my opinion now that all of this secrecy has nothing to do with the supposed advanced nature of OT III. It has nothing to do with the alleged harm it could do to those not qualified or prepared to view it. It's mostly a PR issue.

Hubbard's "wall of fire" incident that the OT III processes address are inarguably strange. But here in 2018, OT III is part of American popular culture. The horses have long left the barn. The continued confidentiality of the material has been rendered pointless and unnecessary. ■

1986 started out like a more or less ordinary year. I had a job, a wife, two kids, and a handful of good friends. Maybe I could leave the turmoil of the past permanently behind me. On Sunday, January 26, we were having a Super Bowl party with a few Scientologists, watching the Chicago Bears clobber the New England Patriots. During the game, Susie got a curious phone call that put a perplexing cast over our festive affair. Susie informed everyone that all Scientologists were being instructed to attend an important briefing on Monday night at the Hollywood Palladium.

What on earth could this could be about? I didn't have a clue, but I was inclined to think it was some bad news, perhaps another legal judgment against the Church. I have a pretty good imagination when I put my mind to it, so I went into all sorts of wild speculation. Maybe the U.S. government had officially outlawed Scientology and we were all fugitives now. Or maybe there'd been some political coup and psychiatrists were now running the country. In the mind of a Scientologist, such things are possible.

On Monday night, Susie stayed home with our son, who was now almost six, and our baby girl who was two months old. I'd be the one to get whatever news there was.

The Palladium was packed by the time I arrived. Several hundred Scientologists were standing outside waiting to get in, but the place was already full. The word was being passed around that Celebrity Center was showing a video simulcast of the event. That wasn't more than a mile away. Most of us just walked over there to avoid parking problems. What a sight to see several hundred people walking through the streets of Hollywood.

Celebrity Center had set up lots of chairs outside with a large projection video screen. I managed to find a seat in what was a standing room only crowd, just in time for the start of the broadcast. David Miscavige, Chairman of the Board of the Religious Technology Center was speaking. He announced that Hubbard had "dropped his body," (a Scientology euphemism for death) and had "moved on to his next level of research."

Hubbard was 74, but I'd never really considered such an inevitability as the end of his life. I was taken by surprise. As a wave of grief was about to overcome me, Miscavige acknowledged the grief we all must have been feeling. He made it a point to emphasize that Hubbard was still engaged in the work he set out to do. He just wasn't doing it in a physical form any more.

Although the news caught me by surprise, I'd actually imagined much worse. When I got home, I think Susie was a bit apprehensive. I gave my son a hug and put him to bed, and said that everything was all right. Then I related the whole event to Susie as best as I could recall.

■ IN RETROSPECT: Scientologists don't accept death as a final state of existence. They believe in past lives (which implies future lives as well). The general agreement among Scientologists is that Hubbard had left his body, left planet Earth, and was now engaged in super advanced OT research somewhere out in the cosmos. It's possible I suppose, but I wouldn't count on it.

I've known a few Scientologists who've speculated on Hubbard's whereabouts, and what he might be doing. Perhaps he's starting a new Scientology movement on some other planet. Or maybe he's devising new OT levels that Scientologists can do in their next life. I've known some Scientologists who've thought about "finding Ron," once they "drop their body."

In truth, the details of Hubbard's death contain a number of conflicting reports. The exact circumstances and precise chronology are vague at best. The same can be said about the turnover of power from Hubbard to top executives in the Church. As usual, the rank and file Scientologists were outside of the loop. ■

Chapter 14

Lessons Not Yet Learned

See Glossary for: *Field Staff Member*

In 1986 we moved into a larger house in a nice suburban neighborhood called Mount Washington, five miles from downtown L.A. My dad had bought the house, and planned for me to pay the rent. His company, Seagate Technology was doing extraordinarily well, and he must have been experiencing quite a surge in wealth. I guess he hadn't entirely written me off for selling all of my stock, though I wouldn't have blamed him if he had. Buying the house was an extraordinary gesture, in light of my recent lapses in financial judgment.

My dad also offered to loan me some money to start a business that I'd been talking about. I'd mentioned that I was considering buying a small printing press and starting some kind of printing operation in my spare time. I wasn't even thinking in terms of a full time venture. I still had my advertising job downtown and was looking for ways to enhance my income. I certainly wasn't expecting any financial assistance.

Besides being the founder and CEO of Seagate Technology, my dad had started a venture capital company and had made a few investments including a charter airline company, a computer repair shop and a patented hi-fi speaker. He proposed loaning me $100,000 dollars which would allow me to start a printing and graphics company. I gladly accepted.

In September, Chris Shugart Studios Printing and Graphics was born.

I should have seen what was coming next, but I didn't. I wasn't aware that Susie had mentioned to someone in the Church that I was starting my own business. When she revealed the amount I was getting, it took less than 48 hours for Church officials to arrive at my front door.

Barry had been our *Field Staff Member* for a few years now and we knew him pretty well. Like all FSMs he performed a valuable service by promoting Church services to Scientologists. He was one among a couple dozen Scientologists who actually made a full-time living selling Scientology.

Barry came over to our house one night to propose an idea. He'd brought along a couple of Church registrars, so I knew a hardball sales pitch was coming straight at me. The three of them recommended that I spend some of my start-up money to go to Flag and do OT VI and VII. It didn't sound like such a great idea.

It seemed to me that I'd be embezzling money for non-business expenses, but Barry didn't see it that way. He was totally confident that what he was proposing was perfectly ethical. I got the same old line that I might get from any registrar: Achieving self-improvement through Scientology would ultimately bring improvement in all of my endeavors—including business start-ups. Barry used the phrase "personnel enhancement" to make the deal sound more legitimate. It still didn't seem right.

In the first place, my dad wasn't keen on my involvement in Scientology. I didn't like the idea of accepting a business loan from him and then give some of the cash to the Church. There was something about it that felt wrong. Besides, how was I going to explain to him that I'd bought some auditing at

Flag and was calling it a "business expense?" Barry had a simple answer for that: "Don't tell him." I didn't like that solution, but the pressure continued.

One of the registrars emphasized that I had the resources in hand to pay for OT VI and VII. It was a fantastic opportunity to make significant spiritual progress. All I had to do was write a check and I'd be on my way. Only an aberrant person would balk at the chance of achieving greater levels of ability and awareness. Rather than succumb to my aberrations, I did the most "rational" thing I could do—I wrote the check and prepared for a trip to Flag.

For any Scientologist, going to Flag is an all-consuming activity. Completing OT VI and starting on VII typically took several weeks at least, and it could take months. Not only did I divert some of my start-up money, I was going to have to postpone my start-up.

I wasn't even in business yet, and here I was writing the Church a check for about $15 thousand dollars. It didn't feel right, but I did it anyway. The source of my misgivings was my reactive mind, I reasoned. Even though the transaction was an emotionally unpleasant experience, I'd convinced myself that ultimately, it was for my own good. One of the earliest entries in my business ledger book reads: "personnel enhancement." Hopefully my dad would never audit my books.

■ *IN RETROSPECT:* When the Church wants you to donate lots of money, they can get into some serious arm-twisting. One common tactic is something critics like to call the "tag team session." It's an apt description of my most recent experience.

Usually a group of two or more will come at you from different directions by rotating from one registrar to the next. It's like getting hit from one side and then the other, and not knowing where the next blow will be coming from. It can break you down emotionally. I've experienced this tactic a few times, and it's never pleasant. Sometimes the same tactic is used for recruiting, and I've read personal accounts where it's been used in Ethics situations too.

Why are Scientologists willing to put up with this abuse? Part of it is indoctrination. Part of it is psychological manipulation. And there's always the bottom line: *eternity*— that irresistible carrot at the end of the stick that always seems to bring Scientologists coming back and asking for more. They're thoroughly convinced that L. Ron Hubbard has provided the only means towards spiritual freedom, immortality, and happiness forever.

Spiritual goals aside, Scientology eventually turns into a duty and obligation that extends beyond your own needs. You have a duty to mankind to bring them their only hope of salvation. Driven by such an immense purpose, Scientologists sometimes get caught up in irresponsible behavior. But as long as the end result benefits Scientology, a lot of unsavory things get swept under the rug.

Church officials can cloud your better judgment simply by invoking the "reactive mind." Because Scientology can successfully handle this irrational mind, anything you do in Scientology is by definition a rational act, and ultimately good. Any impulse that appears to impede or delay one's progress in Scientology is therefore an irrational and harmful manifestation. Using this logic, my reservations and bad feelings were really just a product of my reactive mind, and only served to prove that I needed Scientology. This is Scientology's most insidious and ingenious "catch-22." ▪

I arrived at Flag in late November, right after Thanksgiving, and now I was going through all of the standard paces to begin OT VI. Before getting on to the level, all Scientologists need a certain amount of "setup" auditing. The number of hours varies case by case, but I had paid for 25 hours of OT setups and figured I was ready to go. Part of the process involves a procedure called a Security Check. As I've previously mentioned, the OT materials are confidential and the Sec Check is meant to ensure that those who start an OT level have nothing in their past or background that might compromise the confidentiality of the materials. The Sec Check is also meant to ensure that as a Scientologist, you're not going to be a danger or risk to the Church.

I'd only just arrived when I was informed that I was going to need 50 hours of set up auditing, not the 25 hours I had paid for in L.A. It's common practice to lowball one's auditing estimate in order to encourage advance payments. For example, a registrar might tell you that you need about 50 hours to complete an auditing level. You write the check, and then the Case Supervisor looks at your case folder, and informs you that in you're going to need 100 hours. The CS has the final word, and you can't begin your service until you have your entire estimate paid in full.

I had to be routed back to the registrar. I'd already gone through the trouble of setting aside a chunk of time to do my OT levels and I'd come all the way to Clearwater, Florida to do them. Too late to turn back now. So I gritted my teeth and wrote a check for an additional $10 thousand.

When routing through a Church org you become something like a moving target in a shooting gallery. And everyone wants a shot at you. I had to see the Sea Org recruiter and convince her I didn't want to join. I saw someone in charge of raising funds for a new Flag building that they were financing through individual donations. Somewhere along the way I had to visit the Bookstore Officer. His job was to ensure that I had all of the required materials for whatever it was that I would be doing. You get used to it.

Flag is where you'll typically find your most affluent Scientologists. Consequently, all Flag registrars know that we're big fish in a potentially lucrative pond. There's one organization that exploits this more intensely than any other Church unit. They are the International Association of Scientologists. You can sometimes sidestep some of the items on the routing form, but not the IAS. Speaking to them is just about mandatory.

I was "invited" to attend a "personal briefing," which in Scientology-speak means a meeting with either a registrar or recruiter who will attempt to extract money from you or try to sign you up for a Church staff position. My encounter with the IAS was pretty typical. First I was told that the psychiatric industry was in cahoots with world governments and together they were actively seeking domination over the world. It was all packaged in a way to create profound fear and alarm. Of course, the only solution to such frightening circumstances was to donate huge amounts of money to the IAS. In that moment, the entire fate of the world was being put on my shoulders. The registrar insisted that I needed to take action, and take it now.

What should I do, I asked? I was told sternly that I should donate 20 thousand dollars. I knew how the game worked. IAS registrars always start out by setting their sights high and slowly negotiate their way down to a realistic amount. For me, that amount ended up being $5 thousand. I dutifully wrote another company check and wondered if I was going to have any money left to start my business which didn't even exist yet.

As I worked my way through the Flag routing form, it finally started to look like I'd be getting started on my OT Preparations. I had a brief interview with an auditor who asked me a few general questions about how I was doing in life, if I was encountering particular problems, difficulties, and so forth. The information was then given to the Case Supervisor who would draw up a program designed to get me properly set up. The CS also needed to determine that I didn't have any situations that might make me a potential security risk.

Things seemed to be going smoothly, and I thought I was on my way to starting my auditing program. But there was something that came up regarding my case that made everything screech to a halt. I had a brief meeting with the Director of Processing in which I was told the Case Supervisor had designated me an "illegal PC." In short, I'd become ineligible to receive any auditing because I had a sister-in-law who worked for the FBI.

I hadn't even mentioned this in the interview, and honestly, it slipped my mind. It wasn't an issue so I never thought about it. But it did come up in a previous security check in L.A. and was a part of my official Ethics record. It's standard practice to keep written records of everything that occurs in any Ethics interview. It follows you around like a CIA intelligence dossier. Before a Scientologist begins any auditing program, the Case Supervisor has reviewed your entire case, including previous auditing, Ethics programs, and other interviews.

In my previous auditing, my sister-in-law had never come up as a serious issue. But the Church is wary of Scientologists with government connections because such relationships are considered potential threats of government infiltration. Such scrutiny was Hubbard policy[1], and represented a Church-wide view that world governments were actively involved in trying to destroy Scientology.

My sister-in-law wasn't an agent—far from it. She'd gotten an entry level position working in an administrative department. Nevertheless, this constituted having a family member connected with the government, and the Church was going to enforce the letter of the law. Until further notice, Susie and I were barred from getting any form of Scientology processing.

I discussed my options with the Director of Processing. If Susie and I could somehow convince my sister-in-law to quit her job, that would change things in our favor. While that seemed unrealistic, the other option was even more so. We could sever our ties with Susie's sister and never see her or speak to her as long as she remained with the FBI. In Scientology this is known as "disconnection," a policy that's been responsible for divorces and the breakup of friendships as well as entire families.

They were both bad options, and I said so. Susie was very tight with her family which consisted of six siblings who all lived in our area. Family get-togethers were frequent and severing our ties with them would have been unthinkably outrageous, not to mention heartless and cruel. I tried to imagine my in-laws reaction if Susie and I were to tell them that we weren't going to see them anymore because our Church wouldn't let us. It was an absurd solution not even worth considering.

Yet, as a Scientologist I had a real situation on my hands that needed to be properly dealt with to the satisfaction of the Church. I was now faced with one of the sad realities in Scientology. Some Church members do opt for disconnection and the consequences are always unfortunate. Not only does it disrupt close relationships, but it has great potential for creating animosity among those who aren't Scientologists.

■ *IN RETROSPECT:* I believe that much of the public criticism towards Scientology can be traced to their terribly misguided practice of disconnection. Although the Church has officially cancelled one Policy Letter concerning disconnection, the practice is still much in use. The fact is that in some circumstances, disconnection is unavoidable. There's no way that any Scientologist can remain in good standing as long as they have contact with people antagonistic towards Scientology.

Because this policy has created considerable flak among the public, Church PR has tried to put a positive spin on the subsequent fallout. The official party line is pretty lame. Church spokespeople have replaced the word disconnection with the word "shunning," which is an attempt to give this crude practice an air of legitimacy. By using the word "shunning," the Church believes that they're merely participating in a traditional religious practice accepted and well known through the ages.

The Church defends disconnection by insisting that any individual has the right to associate with whomever they please. Every Scientologist is free to "shun" those they believe would be detrimental to their personal well-being. I don't deny that such a right exists—freedom of association is an important liberty. But the Church has misused and abused this right far beyond what is acceptable in today's society. ▓

There was one more option at my disposal in dealing with my predicament. I could submit a petition to the Senior Case Supervisor International and appeal my status. It was my best option, and in fact my only option as far as I was concerned. I knew I wasn't a security risk to anyone; I just had to convince the Church of that. For now, there wasn't anything further that could be done, so I was sent home to work on my petition.

My stay at Flag lasted a little less than three days. In that span of time it hadn't occurred to me that they had the foresight to collect all their money before anything else happened. And the IAS got some of my money too. I'd spent a total of $30,000

145

for the privilege of finding out I wouldn't be getting any auditing. The money would stay on my account at Flag, of course, and would be available to me whenever I was ready and qualified to proceed. No doubt this is why the Church of Scientology insists on always getting their money first.

Chapter 15

Organizational Follies

To leave Flag properly, I'd have to complete my routing form which would give me Church authorization to go home. When you arrive, all public are required to sign an agreement that states that you won't leave without the signed approval of the Senior Case Supervisor. Although the stated purpose of this is to ensure that all public receive complete and proper service, it sometimes creates problems.

For example, I met one Scientologist who was in the middle of an auditing action but had used up all the hours she'd paid for. She didn't have any more money to continue. The Department of Processing wouldn't let her go home until her auditing was complete. They instructed her to stay and figure out a way to come up with more money. She was calling Scientologists on the phone and running around Flag trying to find someone who'd be willing to give her a loan. I don't know if she was successful, but I was glad I wasn't in that situation.

Leaving Flag can be tricky. If you're not ecstatically happy upon leaving, or if there is any hint of a problem or disagreement with your services, you get sent back into the system. Fortunately for me, I hadn't gotten any service and I was secure in the knowledge that routing out would be relatively easy. I still had to get about a dozen signatures from the various Flag departments, and I felt like I was being scrutinized all the way.

Back in LA, I got to work on my fledgling business, hoping to get it off the ground quickly (though with less capital than I'd started out with). The first thing I did was buy the assets of a printing company owned by Scientologists who operated across the street from the LA Complex. I bought their printing equipment and acquired their customer files made up of print buyers mostly from the L.A. Scientology community. Church members are very much into networking and this would be a great way to get myself into that loop quickly.

In January 1987, Chris Shugart Studios was one month old and gradually getting established. I started getting work from some of the Scientology organizations, departments and units in the LA area. The rest of my printing jobs came mostly from businesses owned by Scientologists.

At the same time, I was also taking steps to resolve my "illegal PC" status with the Church. Susie was doing the same. We submitted petitions to the Senior Case Supervisor International, each of us trying to make the same case that there was nothing in our history or background that would suggest that we were a security risk of any kind.

I also included copies of dozens of commendations I'd gotten while a staff member at Westwood Mission. My track record as a Scientologist was exemplary and I thought it unlikely that my status could remain this way for long. I thought it was just a bureaucratic snag that the Church would soon clear up.

After a few weeks, we got a response from the Office of the Senior Case Supervisor International. Before they'd approve our petitions we'd have to submit to an "implant check." This was essentially a thorough Security Check customized to address our particular situation. The results of this interrogatory, along with our petitions would then be submitted for a final judgment.

■ **BACKGROUND:** The "implant check" is part of the Church's world view that covert enemies are trying to infiltrate Scientology. Hubbard always had a great distrust of institutions of authority, be it the media, medicine, government, or academia. Consequently, the Church has always been on the lookout for government plants, undercover reporters, spies and other covert instigators.

In his book, *Science of Survival*, written in 1952, Hubbard claimed to have uncovered through Dianetics research, the existence of a brainwashing technique he called "pain-drug hypnosis." According to Hubbard, this was a common practice of military and intelligence organizations, designed to create obedient agent provocateurs who could carry out orders forcefully implanted in their minds through a combination of drugs and torture. Hubbard claimed that a PDH victim could carry out even the most despicable of acts and have no recollection of it, and have no memory of having been subjected to the procedure. All Scientologists buy into this world of mind control conspiracies, especially where Scientology might be involved. ■

My implant check would have to be done by a Class 12 auditor, the most advanced classification of auditor there is. It was also a service I'd have to pay for. All corrective and preparatory actions that require an auditor have to be paid for in advance regardless of the reasons they're needed.

The implant check is conducted like a standard Security Check and is done on an E-meter using some of the techniques also found in normal auditing. I was told my Sec Check would take about two intensives of auditing (2 x 12.5 hours). That wasn't a problem since I'd already paid for four intensives from my previous visit. Except now I'd have to use my hours for something other than what I had originally planned.

I was in a bizarre situation. I was going to have to pay for special auditing to establish whether or not I could continue to receive auditing. And there were no guarantees that my petition would ever be approved. But it was my only option, so I went along with the program. I didn't like the situation, but I believed my spiritual survival for all eternity was at stake.

I wasn't aware to what extreme the Church had taken this pain-drug hypnosis thing until I started my implant check. In my first session, my auditor spent about thirty minutes going over some of the things he'd be looking for: possible incidents when I may have undergone hypnosis, psychological manipulation, or other forms of coercion (including pain-drug hypnosis). These experiences, being covert in nature, would be below my conscious level of awareness. Plus, they might have been wiped completely from my memory. Total "Manchurian Candidate" stuff.

My whole life was scrutinized in great detail. Even dreams I had while asleep were not beyond suspicion, as they might indicate evidence of something manipulative but hidden from my consciousness. Four days of interrogation came up with nothing. At the end my final session my auditor told me that he was done. He told me that after submitting my session reports to the Case Supervisor, they concluded that there was no evidence that I'd ever received any "implants" or any other kind of coercive manipulation. I'd just spent thousands of dollars learning something that, intuitively, I already knew.

On the other hand, I couldn't help but wonder what would have happened if the auditor had found something. I would have remained ineligible for auditing. Worse, I would have just spent a lot of money to find that out. At least I was still in the ball game. Now I could go home. Except I'd forgotten that I still had to make my way through the Leaving Flag Routing Form and I'd have to go through the organizational gauntlet.

First stop was the Director of Processing who interviewed me on the E-meter. His job was to see that I was happy with my service, and ensure that nothing was missed during the procedure. I said everything was cool and I was anxious to resubmit my petition. I was ready to go.

I knew something was up when the D of P kept asking me more questions. That could mean only one thing: my meter needle was not "floating." When the needle sweeps slowly and smoothly across the meter dial, it's an indicator that all is well. "Thank you, your needle is floating," is synonymous with saying that the auditing process has reached its successful completion.

If the PC's needle is not floating, there are a number of remedies available depending on the situation. In my case, the D of P pulled out a correction list and started asking me a series of questions, noting the needle reaction after each question. I didn't have to respond to any of the questions, just hear and understand them while the auditor checked it on the meter.

Next thing I knew, I was back in session handling an item that cropped up on the correction list. Originally I was told that my program would only take a few days. Now it was taking more than a week. Fairly typical, really. Length-of-stay estimates are always calculated on best-case scenarios that assume everything goes perfectly well. Scientologists eventually figure this out and redo the math. In actual practice you add one half to twice the amount of your estimated time. For example, if Flag tells you that your stay will be four weeks, you need to readjust that figure to six to eight weeks.

I finally got through the correction list and I felt in pretty good shape. Yet Flag wasn't ready to let me go. What now?

The auditing staff was so anxious to get me started on OT VI and VII that they suggested that I compile my petition right there at Flag, submit it to the Senior Case Supervisor International, and wait for a response. I said no.

I'd been at Flag for more than twice the length of time I'd planned on and I had a business to run at home. There was no way I was going to hang around Flag for however many weeks the petition process was going to take. The staff was holding on to some misguided optimism that my petition could be approved in a matter of days. I told them their expectations were unrealistic.

Flag still wasn't ready to let me go and I was incredulous. There was a small administrative matter I'd have to attend to first. Technically, I was still a potential security risk and my status still unresolved. Apparently, someone in the Church thought there might be some legal exposure regarding my situation. I was given a few documents that I had to read and sign. Essentially, I was attesting for the legal record that I had nothing but positive gains from Scientology processing. I had to sign a disclaimer that anything bad that might happen to me following this point was not the fault of the Church. I also had to sign a waiver that said that I would never sue the Church under any circumstances. I signed the documents without hesitation, though by now I would have signed just about anything, just so I could leave.

To my consternation, my departure was held up yet again. My signed papers had to be notarized first (which by the way, added another day to my stay). The Church had their own Notary Public to handle this; a Sea Org member who was also legally qualified to certify documents. (I guess this sort of thing came up a lot.) Not even in the deepest recesses of U.S. government bureaucracy could I have imagined this much red tape. But I endured it with saint-like patience.

Chapter 16

A Lean Mean Religious Machine

When I named my company Chris Shugart Studios, it was in part, a nod to my musical past and also because I thought the name would fit in with my Burbank surroundings. Essentially it was a small-press print shop that I planned on building into a full service graphic design and production company that focused on direct mail advertising.

From the start, my clientele was predominantly Scientologists, a combination of businesses owned or run by Scientologists, and scores of departments within the numerous organizations of the Church. I also worked with a handful of printing brokers who brought me lots of Church related work. I was printing all kinds of Scientology material for organizations like the L. Ron Hubbard PR Bureau, Dianetics Central Marketing Unit, and the Flag Command Bureau.

Not everything I printed was intended for the general Scientology public at large. Not that it was privileged inside information, just not necessarily geared for the average Scientologist nor the general public. The Hubbard PR Bureau published material about L. Ron Hubbard and made it available to the media, politicians, and public institutions. Central Marketing promoted to the book publishing industry. The Flag Command Bureau issued management related material to Church organizations around the world intended for executives and their staff.

In the case of the Flag Command Bureau, the material was never confidential *per se*, but it was material not intended for the general public. I had a sort of tacit agreement with Church orgs that I'd use discretion and sound judgment in regard to their material. Because I was OT V and a reliable and reputable Scientologist, executives considered me qualified to handle the occasionally sensitive document that might come my way.

Having been a staff member, I was thoroughly familiar with the concept of weekly stats. I was always cooperative with the demands that the 2:00 PM deadline created. Consequently, I got a lot of last minute print jobs for which the orgs could count on me as their printer of last resort.

I frequently worked late hours to finish these last minute jobs. It wasn't unusual to find me working through most of the night, sometimes all the way up to the Thursday deadline. But it was good work and I was glad to get it. I was more than happy to be on the Church's roster of reliable printers, and took pride in my good reputation. The execs I dealt with gained a lot of confidence in my ability to consistently turn out good quality printing, delivered on time without fail.

My work with the orgs allowed me a unique view of the inner workings of the Church that wasn't available to your average Scientologist. It also gave me the opportunity to get to know a few mid-management execs I wouldn't ever meet in the normal course of Scientology activities.

I got along pretty well with the guy who ran the Hubbard PR organization, but he was excessively fussy about printing quality. He regularly rejected jobs that were in any way less than perfect. The public image of L. Ron Hubbard was at stake, and that exec would make no compromises. I had to reprint so many jobs that I finally stopped accepting work from him.

I got tons of work from the Dianetics Central Marketing Unit, including their "industry" newsletter. It was basically sales literature geared towards the publishing business meant to encourage bookstores to keep their shelves well stocked with *Dianetics the Modern Science of Mental Health*. The exec in charge was young, but very reliable. And he seemed really smart, too. You couldn't always count on that within the overall Church organization. Many execs were inexperienced, hastily posted, and often in way over their heads.

Outside of the Church, I did a lot of work for Sterling Management, a prominent consulting firm run by Scientologists using Hubbard management policies. (They received unwanted notoriety by getting mentioned in *Time Magazine* in a 1991 article titled, "Scientology, Cult of Power and Greed.") I also did some printing for jazz keyboardist and celebrity Scientologist Chick Corea. He owned his own recording studio and they regularly enlisted my printing services.

Working with Church management was a mixed bag. They operated across a full spectrum of efficiency, from sharp and savvy, to clueless and incompetent. I learned to deal with them accordingly. Naturally, I preferred working with the execs who knew what they were doing, because I knew that things went smooth when they allowed me to do my job. But sometimes I had to deal with staff who seemed to have no idea how to do anyone's job. It could get pathetic, having to coddle Church staff who were so obviously unqualified. I felt a little sorry for these types because they were sincerely trying their best, and at the same time under immense pressure from senior execs to get the job done.

One printing job in particular illustrates how obsessed Church management could get in the quest to get their products out. Their often single-minded focus could actually work against them when it reached extremes that obscured their common sense.

I was working late one evening, trying my darnedest to meet a deadline. However, the printing job proved to be much more complex than had been described to me. It was simply going to take more time than I'd anticipated. The exec in charge was a young lady in her early twenties who didn't appear to have any grasp of the printing process. I explained to her that she'd given me a difficult printing job that was going to take longer than expected. I guaranteed her that there would be no compromise of quality due to the added difficulty, but it would take more time to finish.

I got my first phone call from the young exec around 10 PM. "How much longer?" she asked. I tried to be optimistic. I said it would be at least another hour, maybe a bit longer. A slight delay by any measure, but this exec had a problem. She'd promised some higher-ups that the job would be finished by now, and these senior execs were demanding that she deliver the finished printing immediately. My explanation was going nowhere. It didn't matter to this exec that I was dealing with a printing process that had to run its course. She just expected me to get it done. What else could I say except that I'd try my best?

It was after 11 PM and I was by myself. By this time, the young lady was calling me every fifteen minutes asking for a progress report. I tried to explain to her that the job was moving along fine, but every time I answered the phone, I had to stop the press, and then restart it again. I was trying to make the point that her calls were making the job take longer. I suggested that instead of making me explain why the job wasn't done yet, it would be much better if I could be left alone to complete the job uninterrupted. Still, I wasn't getting through to her.

The phone rang again twenty minutes later with desperate demands from what was now a frantic and frazzled Church exec. I was getting frustrated. I said, "Every minute I spend on the phone with you, while the press isn't running becomes two minutes added delay." I thought I'd finally made my point. Yet the phone rang again after another twenty minutes. The exec told me she had her Church seniors standing in her office demanding to see the finished job. I was starting to get mad. I said, "The job would be done by now, if I wasn't wasting my time talking to you." I managed to get her off the phone and I got back to work.

Incredibly, the phone rang again ten minutes later. The press was running and the job was proceeding smoothly. I finally got smart and didn't answer it. I knew what I was doing, even if this clueless exec didn't. As the press ran, the phone rang...and rang...and rang. I thought, "What kind of insane person am I working with?"

Finally, the last sheet came off the press, and I finally answered the phone. I also had some good news. "The printing's done," I said. The exec was neither relieved nor glad to hear that. She was bent out of shape because I hadn't answered the phone! She said, "OK, we're coming by to pick it up—right now." Well, there was a problem with that. The ink needed some time to dry before I could trim it down to its finished size.

The evening had turned into such an absurd moment that I'd started taking sardonic pleasure from the tragic comedy. But I was being perfectly honest when I said the job needed some time to dry, otherwise the ink would smear. That didn't seem to register in this exec's mind. She told me that some Church execs would be on their way to pick it up. They'd wait at my shop if necessary. Fine. At least I wouldn't be getting more phone calls. Except now I'd have Church execs hovering over my shoulder asking, "Is it done yet, is it done yet?"

The execs arrived in twenty minutes and they waited and watched me trim the job with my electric paper cutter. They were all young and seemed like babes in the woods. They exuded an air of naïve inexperience that stood in stark contrast to their authoritative looking Sea Org uniforms. Underneath their prestigious looking apparel, all spangled with lanyards, insignias, and epaulets, stood a bunch of awkward kids.

I'd done a spectacular job, especially in light of the immense complexity and the pressure to speed things up. But these harried Church execs expressed no appreciation nor gratitude for my exceptional efforts. Instead, they were only irritated that the job took as long as it did. I sent them on their way, just glad to be rid of them. What a fiasco. On the bright side, the finished product remained one of my best examples of lithographic craftsmanship. But as I often say, "No good deed goes unpunished."

While I was making my way through the trials and tribulations of self employment, Susie managed our household, our two children, and worked as a part time bookkeeper. She also kept the books for my business. In between all of this, she was auditing on OT VII. The procedure is done alone without an auditor and is appropriately called "solo auditing."

OT VII is managed and administered exclusively by Flag, and solo auditors are required to return to Flag every six months to ensure they're applying the procedures properly and remedy any difficulties. It's popularly known as the "six month check-up." Now Susie's time had come.

Although the six-month check-up was supposed to be a short procedure, it sometimes wasn't. We figured anywhere between three and eight weeks. With Susie gone for that length of time, taking care of our kids would be an issue. In September 1987, Andrew was 7 and Janette was almost 2. Because my business usually involved long and often unpredictable hours, it would be impossible for me to manage my business and take care of the household at the same time.

Susie had a good friend in Oregon who offered to help. Cathy lived in a rural area with lots of trees, a creek, and a few pets. We thought it might be a worthwhile experience for our kids to get a taste of life outside of the hustle and bustle of Southern California. Though Cathy wasn't a Scientologist, she agreed to take care of our kids while Susie was at Flag.

Cathy even went to the trouble of flying to L.A. to escort Andrew and Janette back to Oregon. Even though the arrangement looked like it was going to work out, I had reservations. Our children would be away from their parents for what could be as long as eight weeks. I thought that my son was old enough to deal with the temporary change, but I wondered how it was going to affect daughter who was so much younger. I was concerned that this enforced vacation might in some way be emotionally stressful for them.

Susie and I weighed the issues like any loyal Scientologists would. Sure, there might be some minor problems with our children being away from home for such a length of time. But those kinds of difficulties didn't outweigh the vast benefits of Scientology auditing. There was absolutely nothing more important than doing Scientology services, even if you must sacrifice certain aspects of your personal, family or social life.

■ **BACKGROUND:** The way that some Scientologists neglect their children has always been a sore point for Susie and me. Some Scientologist parents have no qualms about relegating their children to low priority status in favor of their own Church activities. It sometimes angered us how easy it seemed for some parents to disregard their children that way.

At one time, some of the children of Sea Org members had become a particular problem. Their parents were usually overwhelmed with work seven days a week, sometimes working 16 hour days. It wasn't unusual for these kids to be away from their parents for months at a time. To deal with this situation the Sea Org established the Cadet Org, which was kind of an ecclesiastical version of *Lord of the Flies*. It was run by the older kids who were either pre-teens or teenagers. These kids were often seen running around the Complex unsupervised, and out of control. I remember that it briefly caused a flap within the Scientology community.

Nowadays the Sea Org won't recruit prospects who have small children, because of the high maintenance involved. I've since learned that married Sea Org staff are discouraged from having children. And there have been cases where Sea Org women who got pregnant have been coerced into getting an abortion. In Scientology, children always seemed to be regarded as an inconvenience. It used to bother me a lot. ▨

In the Fall of 1987, Susie was at Flag, the kids were in Oregon, and I was home alone. I guess we all managed to cope with this temporary family rearrangement. I tried to keep in touch with our children by telephone, talking to them about once a week. During one phone call, Susie's friend Cathy mentioned that my daughter was beginning to call her "mom." I didn't find that as disturbing as I probably should have. The kids seemed like they were doing pretty well. It's not like they were being deprived or mistreated. But they were far from home and family.

The weeks were starting to add up. It was now going on six weeks, and one phone call caused me some distress. I had my little girl on the phone and she said, "Time to come home now." I suppose I should have at least been relieved that a toddler of two years still knew where her home was. But I took it in an entirely different way. It *was* time for her to come home. For a child that young, six weeks must have seemed like a long time to be away from mom and dad. It was a painful

160

moment for me. I put on a happy face and did my best to reassure her that she'd be seeing Mommy very soon. Unfortunately, I had no control over how much longer Susie would be away. She'd be at Flag for as long as it was going to take to complete her program.

Though our family was apart for almost eight weeks, I doubt our kids suffered any lingering trauma. All in all, I think our children adapted to the situation pretty well. In fact, I thought our experience was relatively tame compared to some Scientologists in this regard. On the other hand, I get a few pangs of guilt when I think I might have ever been negligent towards my children even for a moment.

From 1985 and throughout the rest of the Eighties, the International Association of Scientologists expanded their activities, especially in the area of fund raising. In my experience, the IAS registrars were the toughest and most intimidating staff in Scientology. Not only did they not take "no" for an answer, they would occasionally question your dedication as a Scientologist. They also liked to project alarming scenarios about how Scientology's enemies were getting ever closer to destroying the Church. The remedy of course was for concerned Scientologists to donate thousands of dollars to the IAS who would then use the money to stem the tide of all the vicious attacks supposedly taking place.

Although the IAS technically operated independently of the corporate structure of the Church, they'd established a presence in just about every public org worldwide. In a strictly legal sense there may have been no connection between the IAS and the Church of Scientology, but outside of a few parishioner volunteers, the IAS was manned by Sea Org staff. In a very practical sense, the IAS was an important apparatus of the

Church that operated in coordinated conjunction with Church management.

By 1988, IAS staff could be seen everywhere around the LA Complex. They'd rented an apartment building across the street from LA Org. IAS staff would patrol up and down the street in an attempt to round up Scientologists to attend a "special briefing." It was only a matter of time before I would pay them a visit.

The IAS briefing typically consisted of a one-on-one meeting with an IAS registrar. The registrar I met with was an all-business no-nonsense sort of guy. He quickly dispensed with the social pleasantries and got into the nitty-gritty affairs of the Church. He told me that we Scientologists were teetering on the brink of destruction. Without giving any specifics, he said that the Church had powerful enemies who were actively seeking the destruction of the entire Scientology organization.

The registrar then explained how these people were going to go about bringing down the Church. He cited something called the RICO act, or The Racketeer Influenced and Corrupt Organizations act. The RICO Act was passed by the U. S. Congress to enable persons who'd been financially injured by criminal activity to seek redress through the state or federal courts. Originally it was intended to give law enforcement, and private persons, broad power to fight organized crime, mobsters, members of drug rings, gangsters, and so forth.

The reg explained to me that RICO had, over time, resulted in unforeseen applications. For example, corporations had been sued under the RICO Act for allegedly distributing false advertisements. Lawyers, bankers, accountants, and other professionals, had been sued under the RICO Act for allegedly assisting clients in carrying out fraudulent acts.

I was told in very explicit terms that the Church of Scientology was now a major target for the RICO Act. As such, the Church was in grave danger of having all of its assets seized. Consequently, the IAS had launched a campaign to raise enough money to withstand and survive a total confiscation of assets. Although I was given no evidence to back up any part of this, I believed him. I was a veteran Scientologists, and had long since bought into these kinds of conspiracy scenarios.

My briefing wasn't over yet. The reg brought out a small booklet with a yellow cover titled *Brainwashing*. The booklet was an overview and analysis of something called "psycho-politics," which the IAS reg claimed was a reprint from the original Russian publication—supposedly a secret textbook on how to brainwash a population. I was led to believe that the insidious forces who wanted to destroy Scientology were currently practicing the techniques laid out in this booklet. The only thing standing between a totalitarian new world order and a free society was Scientology.

I didn't think to ask how the Church happened to acquire such a subversive publication. I just believed it was true. I implicitly trusted everything and anything that originated from Church officials. I was also thoroughly immersed in the great conspiracy against Scientology. I envisioned a devious and covert consortium of psychiatrists, government leaders, secret police, and corporate overlords who were seeking nothing short of world domination. I believed because I was a Scientologist, I was at risk. If things got really bad, perhaps they'd round up all the Scientologists, and throw us into psychiatric reorientation camps. For me, that scenario was very real.

■ *IN RETROSPECT:* I was always somewhat of a government conspiracy aficionado. Because of my involvement with Scientology, I'd become a full blown conspiracy kook. Most Scientologists sooner or later come to see the world as a network of secret plots, ultimately aimed at putting an end to Scientology. Consequently, I was convinced that we really must be an important movement making a worldwide impact, since world governments were trying so hard to bring us down. L. Ron Hubbard, if nothing else, was one of the great conspiracy theorists of the Twentieth Century.

The "psycho-politics" brainwashing manual I mentioned is an amusing bit of Scientology apocrypha. It's one of those things that many Scientologists know about but never speak of publicly. A few ex-Scientologists have from time to time, tried to trace the source of the manual. It's virtually unknown outside of the Church. Many have speculated that it was written by Hubbard as a means to further his own paranoid view of the world. In any case, it is likely a fabrication, and similar to the sort of conspiracy literature you can find on the internet or in alternative bookstores. ▨

Chapter 17

Turning Up the Heat

See Glossary for: *reg job, postulate*

After five years of solo auditing, Susie finally completed OT VII in October of 1988. The pressure was immediately put on her to begin OT VIII. Church registrars will actually try to convince you to stay at Flag to continue with your next service. If they had their way, no one would ever go home. The push was on for her to move on up to the next level. In fact, the push began a year earlier.

OT VIII was officially released to the public in 1987. Though the level wasn't ready for delivery, pre-sales were being promoted to help finance ship maintenance and operations. As of this writing, it's still the highest auditing level you can attain. Hubbard believed that the material was so powerful and volatile that it could only be effectively delivered away from the crossroads of the everyday world. Towards this end, the Church bought a small cruise liner, refurbished it, and renamed it the *Freewinds*. There was even a contest held to name the ship.

The maiden voyage was scheduled for June of 1988 and expenses must have already been piling up. Refurbishing costs aside, the amount of money for fuel, maintenance and docking had to have been an enormous financial burden, especially considering that no *Freewinds* services were being delivered yet.

A new Church organization was put together called the Flag Ship Org that would promote, deliver and administrate Scientology services aboard the *Freewinds*. In spite of pre-sales, that wasn't sufficient to keep the new ship afloat. In order to meet the huge costs that were piling up, the Church conducted an aggressive campaign for additional donations.

One evening, that campaign came unannounced to our front door. It was an unexpected visit from Barry our FSM, accompanied by an FSO reg. The entourage also included one of the Church's "celebrities" Michael Roberts. For years Roberts cashed in on his one major show-biz credit as the streetwise informant "Rooster" in the TV series *Baretta*. Michael Roberts would later get a bit part in Rain Man as the doctor. (These days, you might see him in a TV commercial every once in a while.)

Susie and I invited this group into our living room knowing full well what was coming. When three Church staff members make a surprise visit, you can bet that you're going to get an aggressive full-court-press *reg job*. First came the "briefing." Briefings in Church parlance are thinly disguised presentations with the purpose of getting you to join staff, pay for services, etc. Staff members never say, "Come into my office, I want to sell you something." The wording is always couched into something like, "I'd like you to attend a briefing on the latest news about..." Oddly enough, most Scientologists knowingly and willingly play along with this well known charade.

There is absolutely nothing pleasant about these kinds of meetings, especially when you don't have the kind of money that's being asked for. Demands for large donations are grueling, arm-twisting affairs that can go on for hours. When the stakes are high, registrars don't give up until they get some money.

The conversation will usually turn into a discussion of your personal finances. How much money have you got? What kind of assets do you have? How much debt can you handle? Your only defense is to try and convince the reg that you're practically destitute, without any financial resources. It's an exaggeration of course, as Scientologists manage to come up with thousands of dollars for services all of the time. They even manage to take time off from their jobs to go to Flag for weeks at a time. Everybody involved knows this. It becomes a battle of wills.

We managed to win the battle, at least this time. But Susie had to convince them that she would make a *postulate* that we would somehow pull in a big chunk of income from somewhere and then donate it to the *Freewinds*. It was a good strategy. In Scientology, a postulate is like a mind-over-matter determination that you'll make something happen. Scientologists believe they have this ability, especially if you're an OT. Our *Freewinds* entourage was obligated to accept Susie's promise that we'd somehow come up the money. Scientologists never challenge or question the OT abilities of another.

■ **IN RETROSPECT:** Because of the Church's constant need for funds, FSMs and Registrars have taken it upon themselves to become self-appointed financial advisors who operate with a confidence that conveys a false appearance of expertise in money matters. It can make you feel like you're dealing with an investment broker from Merrill Lynch. I've since wondered why so many Scientologists are willing to follow this kind of unqualified advice. It's not as if they're helping you assemble your investment portfolio. The purpose is clearly to close a sale. On the other hand, I'd been one of those Scientologists who believed that people in the Church always gave sound financial advice. My trust in Scientology seemed unshakable. ▓

I had a brief opportunity to play a minor role in the launching of the *Freewinds*. I got a call one early Saturday evening. It was one of my printing brokers in frantic need of a printing job for the Church. I was getting used to these kinds of last minute requests and I took them in stride, and I rarely turned them down. Beyond the fact that it was good for my business, I was a loyal group member who could answer the call in most any circumstance.

It was a typical Church project—a last minute rush job. When it comes to printing for the Church, you can almost bet every time that it comes with a horrendously tight deadline. But this wasn't your ordinary Thursday-by-2:00PM deadline. The *Freewinds* was about to set sail on its maiden voyage and they were still in need of some printed material.

The job turned out to be pretty mundane, which was fortunate for me, because that meant I wouldn't be up the entire night. As a slight touch of melodrama I was sworn to secrecy surrounding the job. At the time, everything about the maiden voyage, including every detail of preparation had been designated confidential. That included what I was printing: letterhead and assorted forms of the kind a traveler might find in most any hotel. At the time, the release of OT VIII aboard the *Freewinds* was a huge deal, and I felt like a small part of Scientology history.

During the late Eighties, there was a big push to get Scientologists through their OT levels. Susie and I attended numerous briefings, seminars and meetings all geared towards this goal. Naturally, there was always a registrar present to sign up any prospects that might be ready and willing. And even if they weren't all that willing, the registrars would make their sales pitch anyway. The high sales pressure always made me feel uncomfortable.

Doing services aboard the *Freewinds* requires a huge financial commitment similar to going to Flag. First there's the "OT setups" meant to get you properly prepared. In addition to the compulsory Security Check, an auditor needs to make sure that all of your previous auditing is totally complete. There's also the cost of the OT levels themselves. And there are travel expenses as well as room and board. Then you have to factor in your financial reserves. How long can you afford to be away from your job? A certain amount of financial independence is necessary. Many Scientologists solve this problem by creating their own businesses. Others choose to work for companies run by Scientologists, who are willing to grant special leaves of absence.

Throughout 1988 and 1989, Susie and I were prime Church prospects. My next action was OT VII, and Susie's was OT VIII. This made us the constant target of registrars from Flag and the Flag Ship Org.

In general, all Scientologists get stacks of promotion on a weekly basis in the form of mailers, personal letters and phone calls from nearly every sector in Scientology. The phone calls in particular can get annoying, especially on Wednesday nights. It's not unusual to get several calls from desperate staff trying to get their stats up. Many Scientologists keep their answering machines permanently on, and screen their calls to avoid "phone-in unit" staff promoting the latest briefing, service special, or important event. Even your most devoted Scientology parishioner will sooner or later draw the line as to how much brow beating they'll take.

The issue of the moment was OT VIII which was going to run us about $20 thousand. Although our personal debts were getting larger instead of smaller, that's never a hindrance in Scientology. On the contrary, a large debt is often seen as a badge of honor, and a testament to one's determination to be an active Scientologist. Still, our debts were getting to be a problem.

Our FSM, Barry had a plan. We could borrow money against our house. But there was one difficulty that made the plan more complicated than your run-of-the-mill home equity loan. We owed my dad $180 thousand on the house in the form of a personal loan. Barry told us that according to the loan agent he knew, that wouldn't be a problem. We were assured that we could work around that.

Susie was convinced we could pull it off. I had reservations. We'd already been burned on our Seagate stock deal and the subsequent personal loans fiasco. And I was still feeling guilty about having spent some of my business startup money for Scientology services. I couldn't help but worry that we might be headed for a similar disaster. The fact that my dad (who was already opposed to our involvement in Scientology) would figure into this, only intensified my misgivings.

I told Susie that I had a bad feeling about what we were doing. But in the vernacular of Scientology, I was merely suffering from "an earlier similar incident." My unwillingness to go along with this deal was based on an uncomfortable incident in the past, and had no real bearing on the present circumstance. The "reactive mind" ace-in-the-hole card was again coming into play. My reservations towards creating thousands of dollars in debt were merely an irrational reaction. The "rational" course of action was to just go for it, and never mind about insignificant financial worries.

Scientologists are always encouraged to look at the "big picture." In this view, money problems are insignificant, even trivial when compared to the infinite gains one achieves through Scientology. I have to admit, there was a certain liberating experience in throwing caution to the wind. For a moment in time, I could feel free from the constraints of conventional financial realities. Moreover, I believed spiritual reality was always senior to material considerations.

For the eager Scientologist, getting the money for services becomes paramount to other concerns, even standard financial procedures. A home loan was going to take some time, which would be a problem for the Church, which always has their 2:00 PM deadline to factor in. We'd gotten used to this kind of mania, and it seemed like any other normal activity.

To acquire the necessary cash, we first took out a short term, high interest $50 thousand loan using our house as collateral. That would satisfy the Church's time frame. Meanwhile we would proceed with the home equity loan, and once it was finalized, we'd pay off the first debt. We were assured that we could pull this off without a hitch.

We closed the loan deal, and the Church got their money. The next step was to work out the details of the home equity loan. We immediately ran into a snag. In order to get a bank to approve a loan against the equity in our house, I'd have to get my dad to sign a subrogation agreement that gave the bank first priority in any proceedings involving a default on any loans on the house.

Maybe it would only be a minor snag. Susie was optimistic that we'd be able to do this. I wasn't so sure. Besides, I didn't want to get caught up again in any financial entanglements with my dad. Susie said that she'd take care it. That was fine with me. We had to do something in any case. We had $50 thousand dollars to pay off and only thirty days to do it.

Under the guise of "reorganizing our finances," Susie got in touch with my dad and briefly laid out our financial plan. The reorganization aspect wasn't a total lie, but it was definitely only half of the truth. Part of the loan would be used to pay off a major chunk of our credit card debt, taking advantage of the lower interest rate of the equity loan. Half of the loan would be earmarked for OT VIII, plus "set-up" auditing for me to get started on OT VI and VII.

After some casual back and forth conversations, Susie sent my dad some papers to sign. One night I got a call from him. He said he'd looked over the papers and thought the whole thing looked suspect and he wasn't going to sign them. Although he didn't come out and voice his suspicions about our home loan gambit, I knew I was busted. He didn't accuse me directly of being dishonest about the loan, but he let me know wherein his suspicions lied. Out of the blue he told me that he'd recently donated money to an organization whose purpose was to "put Scientology out of business."

I asked him to be more specific, but he wouldn't give me any details. At this point it didn't really matter. In the eyes of the Church, my dad's gesture officially made him an anti-Scientologist. It was one of the worst days of my life.

The revelation contained dire ramifications: Should my dad continue to maintain his anti-Scientology stance, I'd have no other option than "disconnection." If I were to remain a Scientologist in good standing, I'd have no other choice but to sever all ties with him. Up until now, I'd successfully avoided severe confrontations with family members. My good fortune had run out.

I'd hit a low point in my life. Maybe the lowest. For two days I was absolutely dismal. My world had turned into a quagmire of difficult complications with no easy solutions. Would I have to disconnect? I still owed my dad money on my business. How would I deal with that? And Susie and I still had to come up with a way to pay off the $50 thousand short term loan.

I felt awful about pushing my relationship with my dad beyond tolerable limits, perhaps even beyond my ability to repair. I wasn't sure if it was something I'd ever salvage. And I was angry at myself for getting caught up in another stupid situation. Here I was, once again, at the short end of bad advice from Scientologists, and once again holding the bag. Why wasn't I learning from my mistakes?

Barry was very contrite, as he felt partly responsible. But he also said that he'd been misled by his financial associate. Barry promised that he'd do what he could to help clean up the mess.

First, I'd have to restructure what was essentially an unsecured loan. So we set up a "hard money" loan, which works very much like a credit card debt. In addition to a very high interest rate, we'd also be paying back some principle, and after two years, there'd be a final balloon payment. The balloon payment would be a new problem to solve down the line, but we'd at least bought ourselves some time to work something out.

There was also the issue of my dad. The Church takes a hard line on friends and family members who are antagonistic towards Scientology. A member who is connected to anyone hostile to Scientology is labeled a "Potential Trouble Source" and isn't allowed to do any training or auditing as long as the issue persists.

Per Scientology policy I had two options. I needed to somehow handle any antagonism my dad might have towards me and the Church. If I was unsuccessful doing that, then I'd have to disconnect. Both options seemed tricky and complicated. I wasn't sure how to approach my predicament.

Barry gave me some advice that I wasn't ready for. "Go see him and talk to him," he said. "Like, right away?" I asked. "Get on the phone right now and tell your dad that you want to see him," Barry said in a matter-of-fact sort of way.

I had to admit, the idea was simple and straightforward. I had no clue as to what I might say, but it did seem like it might be the best course of action. So I began making arrangements. I called my mom and step-dad in San Jose and told them we were taking a short vacation and would be spending a couple of days with them. I then called my dad and said I wanted to drop in. Everything was set. We left our kids with some good friends in L.A. and caught a flight to San Jose, not knowing what our encounter might bring.

When Susie and I met with my dad, he was cordial and friendly. I figured he had a general idea what was on my mind, but if so, he didn't let on. It would be up to me to get the ball rolling.

I hadn't thought out what I was going to say. I figured if I was just honest and straightforward the conversation would naturally move in the direction I wanted it to go. So I just laid my cards on the table. I said, "It seems to me that lately you and I have found ourselves sitting in opposing enemy camps."

My dad smiled and said, "Yeah, I guess that's true."

I said I felt I was in an untenable position. I was committed to Scientology, yet feared it was creating a rift between us.

My dad made it clear that he had no problem whatsoever with my beliefs. His problem was with how the Church conducted its business with me. He thought their constant push for donations was deceptive and the amounts they demanded were excessive. While I was willing to acknowledge that to an outsider it might appear that way, I saw Scientology as something that was making important contributions to the improvement of society.

Never one to shy away from expressing a frank opinion, he said, "I think Scientology is bad for the world." I had no intention of turning the conversation into an argument about the worth of Scientology. I just hoped that my dad would understand where I stood. For him I suspect it was much the same. The bottom line was we had a disagreement that we probably couldn't resolve, and we'd both have to decide whether or not we could live with it. To use a diplomatic term, I guess we'd reached a tenable level of *détente*.

Because of this fiasco, I think I was at least beginning to learn from my mistakes. I resolved to be completely honest about my Scientology activities even if it wasn't necessarily in the best interests of the Church. It dawned on me that perhaps I'd been compromising my own integrity for the sake of Scientology.

Chapter 18

Lifestyles of the Faithfully Devoted

Scientology is a *workable system*. So says Hubbard and his loyal followers. This doesn't mean it's the best possible system or a perfect system. That concept had taken on a new meaning for me. Scientologists had flaws like anyone else. They weren't perfect, and certainly could make mistakes like anyone else. Our intentions were good, even if our methods were occasionally flawed.

■ **IN RETROSPECT:** In spite of our many setbacks, Susie and I managed pretty well holding things together. We never let our mishaps get so out of hand that we lost control of our lives. Ironic perhaps, but we attributed our ability to overcome our problems to our knowledge in Scientology, the very thing that was creating those problems in the first place. But when you're a devoted Scientologist, it can turn into a self-perpetuating game that never ends.

By now I was a veteran Scientologist of many years, and there was one thing that was simply beyond dispute: Scientology could handle any problem in life whatsoever and without exception. All Scientologists eventually become convinced of this.

This kind of absolute certainty produces a wicked circle that puts Scientologists on an endless treadmill. It works this way: When Scientology auditing or training doesn't produce the expected result, the solution is more auditing and training to correct whatever didn't work. In this way, Scientology operates simultaneously as both the problem and the solution.

Scientology can be a perpetual cycle that can go something like this:

Why aren't you on course?
"I don't have enough time, I'm too busy right now."
You need to take a course that will teach you how to handle your time more efficiently.

Why aren't you doing your next auditing level?
"I don't have the money to pay for it."
You should come in and do a course on how to deal with money problems.

When a Scientologist is doing poorly on their training or auditing, there are remedies designed to repair whatever went wrong. If a Scientologist becomes dissatisfied with a service, there's a corrective action for that. Even if you decide that you don't want to be a Scientologist any more, there's a remedy that's designed to keep you in the Church. Regardless of the difficulty, there's one, and only one option: more Scientology.

This is the world that Susie and I had become an integral part of—a self-contained universe that exists for and unto itself. Our primary goal in life had become to "move up the bridge." Everything we did was determined by how it would allow us to do our next training or auditing level. And when we weren't moving up the bridge, we were expected to help and encourage other Scientologists to remain as involved as possible.

Scientologists believe without question that Scientology is the only hope for mankind. There is simply nothing else. They also believe that their activities contribute profound benefits that are unprecedented in the history of the world. In the autumn of 1989, that is what Susie and I believed. ■

Now that Susie had OT VIII paid for, we had to make family arrangements. Our kids were 9 and 3 now, and I thought I could manage my business and at the same time be a temporary "single" dad. They both went to a private school run by Scientologists, who could care for them until 6:00 PM. If I had to work late, a former employee was available to take up the extra work or even watch the kids.

Meanwhile, Susie made travel arrangements. She would first fly to Clearwater and do some auditing set-ups as well as a Security Check at Flag. Then she'd fly to Puerto Rico and to the island of Aruba, part of the Netherlands Antilles where the *Freewinds* had its home port.

By Scientology standards, OT VIII is relatively short, usually just a couple of weeks. Most of Susie's time was spent doing a course between auditing sessions. Susie went through the system without a snag and was finished in the short time predicted.

I managed the home front, juggling my business demands with those of my kids. It was a little stressful at times, but knowing it was temporary made it tolerable.

Susie got back soon enough and life resumed to its normal pace. Susie said she had a great time and that OT VIII was a great level. Of course, it had to have been a great level. If it wasn't, she'd still be on the ship working it out until she could attest to glowing results.

To be honest, I didn't notice any remarkable difference. As a matter of fact, I had doubts that even her OT VII auditing the year before had done her any good. But by this time, I was smart enough to keep my mouth shut. If nothing else, I was learning in Scientology how to stay out of trouble.

The year 1990 was my best year business-wise. I was getting a lot of work from many of the Church organizations as well as from businesses run by fellow Scientologists. One of my best customers was a broker who funneled me work from Scientology-related organizations. Towards the end of the year, I decided to close my shop down and go to Flag to start OT VII.

The OT levels are done by "invitation only" and are granted to the PC by the Case Supervisor. In order to be eligible for OT VII, I'd have to undergo a Security Check using the e-meter. Any indication of anything even slightly out of the ordinary would have to be taken up with an Ethics Officer.

The contributions one makes as a group member is another factor that determines one's eligibility. You're expected to be an active Scientologist above and beyond just showing up for course or session. The Church expects you to be an FSM promoting Church services to others, and to be an active participant in Church-related activities in the community. Once all this gets factored in, the Senior Case Supervisor decides whether you're worthy.

I arrived at Flag right after the Thanksgiving weekend and immediately got into the routine of a full-time student. It's a grueling schedule, day and night, seven days a week. With the exception of Sunday mornings, I was on course from 9:30 AM to 10:30 PM. I pursued it willingly, believing my hard work would result in substantial progress towards OT.

I planned to get all my set-up and eligibility procedures done (this was called OT VI), which would take a couple of weeks, and then come back a few months later to start OT VII. This piecemeal approach wasn't unusual for Scientologists who couldn't set aside big chunks of time to do everything from start to finish.

When two weeks was just about up, I was ready to leave. The problem was, I hadn't quite finished. It was now the middle of December, getting close to Christmas, and my room and board expenses were starting to add up. I wanted to be home with my family for the Holidays. I was also worried about leaving my business unattended for so long.

When I talked to the course supervisor about this, she opposed my leaving. (I'd be depriving her of substantial "student completion points.") Although I tried to convince her I had every intention of coming back in a couple of months, I should have known my plan wasn't going to fly. Course completions are the most important products a supervisor has, and they figure enormously in calculating weekly stats.

I was "on the grid" as they say in Scientology orgs. That means that the Dept. of Training had me targeted to finish by the end of the week, and that meant a significant boost to their stats. If I were to leave, their production stats would be adversely affected.

I put up a bit of a fight, but in the end, I got talked into staying. How could I, in good conscience, be responsible for messing up the training department's stats for the week? I decided to bite the bullet and gut it out. I got home five days before Christmas.

By 1991, Susie and I were well established as part of an elite class of Scientologists. As an OT VIII, Susie was expected to be at all times in the forefront of Church activities. A brand new event revolving around the *Freewinds* was organized to encourage all Scientologists everywhere to "move up the bridge and go OT."

OT VIIIs celebrated the *Freewinds* maiden voyage every June. They'd spend a week or two on the ship, participating in assorted gala events, seminars and a "personal special briefing" by senior executives of the Church. Though the Anniversary Voyage wasn't labeled a mandatory event, it was implied that all OT VIIIs should attend. In spite of that, Susie never went. We just couldn't afford it. Her absence was frowned on by a few higher-ups, but I don't think she ever suffered any serious fallout.

A new group called the OT VIII Committee was organized to promote Scientology to Church members and to the general public. The thinking was that those at the top of the "bridge" were important opinion leaders within the Scientology community. There was another factor in play as well. The Church believed that because of their advanced status, OT VIII's shared a large responsibility to forward the aims of Scientology.

As the husband of an OT VIII, I had many opportunities to hang out with the most advanced Scientologists in the Church. In addition to those I already knew, I had the chance to meet others at a number of events coordinated by the Flagship Org.

I attended these events, but never really enjoyed them. They bored the life out of me. Everyone was always pleasant, but I found the affairs dreary. It seemed I had nothing in common with anyone except for the obvious fact that we were all Scientologists. The conversations always revolved around Church activities. Occasionally you might talk about your job or your business, but that would eventually gravitate towards how you were going to get closer to starting your next Church service.

■ *IN RETROSPECT:* Only now as I look back can I see the transformation that takes place with Scientologists who've been devoted members over many years. There's a subtle homogenization that takes place that gives them a bland similarity. It's a curious paradox, because one of the claims that Dianetics and Scientology makes is that through processing one restores ones individuality. In effect, you become more "you." However, when Scientologists get together, they all sound alike.

Scientologists have an unshakable certainty that with Scientology you can find an answer or solution to every problem, difficulty, or undesirable situation that man has ever encountered. Therefore, a discussion of politics, society, and world affairs becomes redundant and unnecessary. Scientology is the answer. What more does one need to say?

By 1991, I'd come to realize that I didn't really enjoy hanging out with OTs as a group. It was just dull.

I think maybe a part of me always believed there was something more to life than just Scientology, but I also knew it would have been politically incorrect to say so. Perhaps I wasn't quite the fanatic I thought I was. ▧

In spite of my tepid feelings about the OT VIII community, I considered myself a part of it, if only by marriage. I was sort of an "OT VIII-in-law." I still believed everything the Church did was towards a greater good, even though I had reservations now and then. I was still a good soldier fighting the good fight.

The recently established International New OT VIII Committee (INOC) had been put together to help promote the OT levels. One of the first things they did was publish a newsletter for their fellow VIIIs. I was given the task of designing, producing and printing it. Charlie, an OT VIII, volunteered to be the editor. Over several months, we put out three issues which were all well received.

As Charlie and I geared up for Issue #4, we had no reason to doubt it would be another success. However, strange backroom politics were afoot about which Charlie and I were completely in the dark. He'd submitted the editorial material to the Committee for final approval while I waited for their OK. Weeks passed without a word. Neither of us had a clue as to why the delays. The answer eventually presented itself in a rude and sudden way.

One day without warning or fanfare, The *INOC Newsletter Issue #4* arrived at my home. I was dumfounded. Who designed it? Who printed it?

I looked for publishing credits and discovered that one of the Committee members had designed it, and it seemed obvious to me, was not a graphic designer. The articles were so bland and pedestrian I knew that Charlie hadn't written them. Charlie had a pleasant and witty flair for writing that made the newsletters fun to read. This newsletter was awful.

I called Charlie, hoping he had some idea on what the hell had happened. He was as clueless as I was. He told me he'd make some calls and get back to me.

When he called back, he was still a little confused, but at least he had an explanation. Apparently a handful of Committee members were in on this commandeering of the newsletter. Though Charlie wouldn't give me any names, I had a pretty good idea of one. *Issue #4* was printed by a shop owned and operated by an OT VIII Committee member. I was livid.

Outraged and insulted, I got on the phone with Meri, the Committee Secretary. I was prepared to verbally incinerate her, and anyone responsible, but Meri managed to cool me down. She understood my anger and acknowledged that the situation hadn't been handled correctly. Then she apologized on behalf of the Committee and asked me to send her a written report.

I took advantage of the opportunity to vent my spleen on official communication lines. I wrote up my report and sent one to Meri, Charlie, and the INOC exec in charge of ethics matters. In my report I called *Issue #4* amateurish, and accused INOC of slighting my reputation by turning out such a poor product. I also demanded an explanation to why the newsletter job was taken from me, and why I was never informed.

I never got an answer. It turns out that Meri's apology on the telephone was nothing but hollow words. It was the last time I would ever hear anyone speak of the matter, and I never designed or printed another INOC newsletter.

I resigned myself to the fact that I'd lost a graphics and printing client as the result of inside political maneuverings of a few INOC members. I told Charlie I thought the Committee wasn't much more than a "pal-ocracy," of selfish OTs.

Although the incident was clearly underhanded and even devious, I knew that in the grand scheme of Scientology, my shoddy treatment would amount to nothing. The newsletter continued without me, and never came close to reaching the professional quality that Charlie and I had achieved. It was evident to me that quality didn't matter as much to INOC as their desire to work exclusively with their fellow OT VIIIs. In this sense, the INOC group was no different than any other exclusive group of elites.

I never again held OT VIIIs in any kind of special regard. As far as I was concerned, an OT VIII was just another Scientologist who happened to have spent more money for the privilege.

OT VII was still on my list of things to do. But due to some technical revisions, I'd have to do some new auditing rundowns that were part of a revamped OT V. I still had unused auditing hours at Flag that I'd originally paid for as part of my auditing preparations. I was given the impression that I could get this all done with what I had on account. So in September of 1991 I returned to Clearwater, Florida.

Getting auditing at Flag can be a lengthy process. The demand for auditing far exceeds available trained auditors. It's not unusual to wait all day before getting a single session. So when I found myself getting numerous sessions every day, I was happily surprised.

Things were progressing well. So well in fact that I wasn't aware how fast I was using up my auditing hours. But I found out soon enough. One morning, all ready for my next session, I was handed a routing form to see the registrar. Oops—I'd completely run out of hours and no one had seemed to notice. It was supposedly an oversight. The Case Supervisor should have determined beforehand that my "tech estimate" would require that I purchase more hours before I started. But everyone was so eager to get me into session that Church policy had apparently been overlooked.

I suddenly found myself in a fairly common predicament at Flag. I was out of auditing hours, yet I was in the middle of an auditing action. In spite of the accounting error, the Case Supervisor wasn't going to allow me to go home until I completed what I'd started. There's really only one option in a situation like this—pay for more auditing.

Unfortunately, I didn't have the nine thousand dollars to pay for an additional 12.5 hours. I called Susie and explained the situation. By this time we were old hands at creative financing, Scientology style. We had a number of credit cards with substantial credit limits, and I was pretty confident we could come up with the cash.

I'd gotten used to taking on large chunks of debt, but that didn't make it any less exasperating. I racked up an additional nine grand on a credit card, and I'd worry about dealing with the additional debt later. For many Scientologists, this procedure turns into something like a conditioned response. It's as if every time a registrar asks you for money, your hand subconsciously goes for the credit cards in your wallet.

My auditing continued, and that was the important thing. Scientologists accept the fact that services are expensive, and my situation wasn't that unusual. But it's strange how easy it is for Scientologists to go along with the additional expenses they always have to deal with.

Chapter 19

Is There a Way off This Treadmill?

1992 was a slowdown year on several levels. My business had slacked off, the L.A. economy was in decline, and Susie and I were hardly doing any Scientology. Auditing-wise, Susie had gone as far as she could, I no longer had any money on account at Flag, and we were saturated with debt. Our shaky financial circumstances required us to regroup, and focus on paying off the debts we'd acquired over the years. Our constant donations to the Church had finally caught up with us.

There was no more money to be had, through creative financing or otherwise. Keeping my business afloat was now my first priority, and I continued to work long and unpredictable hours. Susie continued at her part time bookkeeping job while managing the household and kids.

Our life had fallen into the monotonous routine that just about every Scientologist eventually gets into. You work, pay off debts, work some more and donate more money to the Church. It's a cycle with no end. Everything you do revolves around how it's contributing to Scientology. And even when you're not making money contributions, or not doing services, you're expected to remain active. You can attend free seminars, briefings, and so forth, and just as important, you can promote Scientology to others.

In spite of our lack of Church activities, the IAS continued to take an active interest in our lives. We'd occasionally get phone calls from IAS registrars asking for more money. They're never concerned whether or not you have any money, and they'll take your last penny or dry up your last asset and call it a good thing.

An IAS registrar called one night and sounded desperate for money. This reg had Susie on the phone for a noticeable length of time and clearly wasn't taking no for an answer. You're wasting your time trying to convince these people that you're broke. This never-say-die IAS reg had an idea. We could sell our television for a couple hundred dollars and donate that money to the IAS! Susie had the good sense to decline such an off-the-wall suggestion.

How can you take people like that seriously? Well, you can't. You can only try to humor them. These were the kind of staff members the Church was using for phone solicitors, and I felt sorry for them. Their desperate attempts to squeeze nickels and dimes out of their fellow Scientologists was embarrassing. Yet at the same time, I understood the mindset.

During one such phone call, I finally asked the IAS reg, "How long are you going to let this conversation drag on until you accept the fact that I'm not going to give you any money?" He ignored my question and continued with his tedious harangue. That was it for me. I said, "This conversation can no longer serve any purpose. I'm done talking to you." Then I hung up.

To my surprise, he didn't call back. What do you know? My audacious tactic actually worked. It was an eye-opening lesson for me: Just say no. What a revelation. I felt like I'd learned a Jedi mind trick that made me invincible.

In spite of my new-found assertiveness, I wasn't totally immune to persuasion. I could still be prodded into compliance if I was convinced the circumstances were warranted. In that context, the IAS were the masters of making compelling cases. They attempted to make their case to me one late Wednesday night.

The doorbell woke Susie and me up. I sat up at 1:30 AM and was momentarily surprised, but I had a sneaking feeling about who might pay us a visit so late at night. I looked out the window and saw Bridgett, an IAS registrar who Susie and I knew fairly well standing on our porch.

Susie asked, "Are you going to let her in?" I didn't think I had much choice.

I let Bridgett in, she apologized for the late visit, then immediately went into her pitch. It was pretty much the same old emergency: the IAS desperately needed money, the Church is under attack, we need your help, yadda, yadda, blah, blah. I wasn't paying that much attention. My thoughts were focused on how I could get rid of her in the shortest amount of time for the least amount of money.

Susie gave Bridgett our dismal financial picture, and mercifully, Bridgett seemed to buy it. Her visit only cost us $250, debited off of one of our many deep-in-debt credit cards. A dubious victory, to be sure, but I just wanted to go back to bed.

I was becoming aware of an odd paradox that I had trouble reconciling. On one hand, saving the world was an expensive proposition. That much I'd accepted. But how was I going to create and maintain my own prosperity? Any time I might come into a period of economic affluence or experience a momentary financial windfall, the Church would be there insisting they get their portion of it—as large a portion as possible.

If it wasn't Flag, it was the IAS. Or it could just as well be the dozens of other Scientology projects that were constantly in need of donations. I was struck with the unsettling notion that no matter how much money I made, the Church would always be there trying to get their share. I felt like I was on a treadmill, and I needed to figure out a way to get off it.

Like many Scientologists, Susie and I drove beat up old cars rather than buy new ones. We also avoided buying new home furnishings, getting by with old and worn out furniture and family hand-me-downs. And as with so many Scientologists, most of our discretionary income went to the Church. I once said to Susie, "How can I continue to be motivated to create a prosperous business when I never get a chance to enjoy the fruits of my labor?" Susie had to admit that most of our extra income was either going to the Church, or going towards paying off Church related debts. The Church of Scientology money-go-round was wearing me down, and I wondered if there was a way off this expensive carousel.

Throughout 1992 my business remained sluggish due in part to the stagnant L.A. economy. Several large national corporations were moving out of the area and relocating to more business-friendly cities. I'd also read in an article about the film industry—an economic mainstay of Southern California—that several movie production companies were leaving the area. It got me to thinking maybe I should consider relocating as well.

The L.A community suffered a traumatic blow at the end of April. Four cops were acquitted for the beating of Rodney King, and rioting spread throughout South Central L.A. and vicinity. The damage was alarming: 53 deaths, 2,300 injuries and 10,000 arrests. About 1,000 buildings were destroyed amounting to over $1 billion in damages. As I was leaving my shop out in Burbank, I could smell the smoke from twenty miles away.

As distressing and sobering as the riots were, I believed that the community would eventually recover and rebuild. Unfortunately, some events that followed gave me the impression that I might be wrong. Spokespeople for the black community were speaking out in defense of the rioters, especially the ones who nearly killed Reginald Denny and were now facing criminal charges. On one hand, black leaders were decrying lack of jobs in the inner city, but on the other hand were trying to justify the riots that had destroyed so many local businesses. It made no sense. The economic damage that the rioters had created only put whatever jobs were available that much further out of reach.

The Los Angeles City Council put together a "rebuild L.A." program that was designed to encourage business people to build new commercial establishments in South Central L.A. To help fund this program, the city raised business license fees by $10. Had the LA City Council lost their minds? It wasn't so much the $10, as it was the City Council's backwards thinking process: attract more business by making it more expensive to get one started. It sounded crazy.

Up to this point, I'd tolerated the taxes and regulatory fees. I'd tolerated the bureaucratic procedures the city made small businesses run through, and I was willing to weather the economic hard times. But I'd finally reached my limit.

I'd never had strong feelings of dissatisfaction with Los Angeles. I knew people who'd spend years scheming ways to get out, but I wasn't one of them. I actually liked L.A. Now that attitude was changing.

I started writing inquiry letters to chambers of commerce, business development groups, and anyone else looking for businesses to relocate to their city. The response I got was impressive. I received over a dozen portfolios and other literature from all over California, and a few more from other states in the West. I saw nothing but opportunity.

I came home one evening and declared "We're moving."
Susie asked, "Where?

I didn't have a concrete plan, but I was determined to see this through. I said, "We need to move out of L.A. I don't know how or when, but we gotta do it."

Maybe the City Council hadn't lost their minds. Maybe it was me. Susie certainly thought so.

She humored me through my manic moment without actually telling me she thought I was treading towards the deep end. Susie had a habit of airing our problems with our FSM, Barry, who occasionally served as a sort of mediator and counselor when we were having difficulties. Rather than argue with me, she called him.

I got a call from Barry the next day. He told me Susie was concerned about my grand pronouncement and that she felt that it was an idea headed for disaster. I tried to reassure him that although I may have made it sound like a crazy idea, I was serious nevertheless. I told him I'd try to smooth things out. So I repackaged my idea in a way that made it sound more level-headed. I don't know if Susie bought it, but at least she didn't think I was crazy anymore.

In September 1992 we attended a wedding in Pebble Beach where one of my dad's stepdaughters was getting married. At the ceremony, I met a man named Mort, who was a friend of my dad's. We had a brief and casual conversation in which I mentioned that I was into graphic design and printing production.

Several weeks later I get a phone call from Mort at my Chris Shugart Studios office. He told me he might need some freelance graphics work from time to time. I briefly outlined my specific capabilities and told him that I'd send him some samples.

In January 1993, I decided to abandon my printing operation and focus on graphic design. I had no idea if it was a good marketing move, but at least it was a practical one. I was slowly going broke and it wasn't getting better. I'd sell all my printing equipment, reorganize, and reinvest in an exclusively graphics oriented operation. If nothing else, it would buy me some time to stabilize my wobbly finances.

Maybe I was just jumping out of the frying pan and into the fire. But sometimes good fortune smiles on us for no apparent reason other than your being in the right place at the right time.

One afternoon my dad called with a business proposal. As it turned out, Mort, the man I met at the wedding was putting together the Carmel Bay Publishing Group in partnership with my dad. He needed someone with expertise in both graphic design and printing production. That was me.

My dad suggested I could move up to the Monterey Bay area and work for the new company. He told me to think about it and added, "Of course you'd probably have to sell all your equipment first."

I laughed to myself at the serendipity.

I was flabbergasted, but in an exciting way. It was a promising opportunity, and I was attracted to the prospect of moving to Monterey. Besides being a beautiful area, I considered it a sort of home away from home. I'd grown up in San Jose, and the Monterey Bay area was a familiar stomping ground from my youth. But there were some practical considerations concerning the logistics of moving a business, a home and a family. There were financial considerations. How exactly was I going to make money in this new venture? In spite of all that, I was sold on the idea.

Now came the real task. How do I sell the idea to Susie?

For the time being I kept my dad's conversation to myself. Making specific plans would have been premature. For the next month I was in touch with Mort and we discussed back and forth some details and terms of my prospective new employment. I wrote up a plan that included a few salary options. At the same time, I began to broach the subject with Susie, trying to make it sound purely theoretical and speculative. She was skeptical, but at least she wasn't telling me what a hare-brained half-assed idea it was. Fine, I'd go with skeptical.

In March my dad gave me the go-ahead to start putting the whole deal in motion. Now came the moment of truth. I had to convince Susie we were moving to Monterey. I laid out as specifically as I could how I thought we could remain financially solvent while the whole relocation process was in progress. It was going to be tight, but it was doable—just barely.

I don't think Susie embraced my idea with the same enthusiasm I had. She was more cautious than I, but she knew me well enough to know when my mind was made up. This was one of those times. For better or worse, we were moving to Monterey.

Chapter 20

The View From Afar

In the summer of 1993 I sold my printing equipment, gave notice to my Burbank landlord, and stored the rest of my office stuff in my garage at home. We put our house up for sale and spent two weeks in July looking for a house in Monterey. I also started drawing a salary from Carmel Bay Publishing.

In spite of past conflicts and friction between me and my dad, he was willing to help me buy a house, and he trusted my professional abilities. However I suspected that at least a part of his motivation in my relocation was to keep me out of trouble. I'm sure that he was aware as much as I was that living on the Central Coast would significantly weaken the gravitational pull of Scientology.

I couldn't deny that my relationship with the Church was going to change. Leaving L.A. would put some distance between me and Scientology. Scientologists outside the major Church centers are less exposed to the daily pressures to donate money, get in session, get on course, and be so thoroughly involved. It felt good.

We had a going-away party before the move. The guests were mostly Scientologists, including our IAS registrar Bridgett, and a couple of other Sea Org staff. The following week we packed up our two cars, and the Shugart family headed for Monterey. With all of our worldly belongings in tow, and rapidly running out of money, I felt like a character out of Steinbeck's *The Grapes of Wrath*, especially as we entered the Salinas Valley.

Monterey was home now, and I couldn't have been happier. I'd gotten out of L.A. and away from the constant presence of the Church. Still, I had no real desire to sever my ties entirely. Monterey actually had a Scientology mission for a while and so did Salinas. (Both eventually closed due to lack of support.) There were a handful of Scientologists living in the area and it would only be a matter of time before Susie and I would connect with our new and smaller Church community.

"Staying connected" is an important concept in Scientology. Church members make it a point to keep in touch with their fellow parishioners. Northern California had a number of Church organizations including liaison offices for Flag and the IAS. These two organizations were very active in keeping the more remotely located Scientologists in touch and involved.

The nearest Church to us was the Stevens Creek org in San Jose. It was about an hour and a half drive, so we were seldom there. But there were about a dozen or so Scientologists scattered throughout our area and every now and then a Flag representative would organize a get-together. It was the usual push to get us to do more services, but there seemed to be less pressure.

In 1995 the Flagship Org initiated a new promotion. Typically, the *Freewinds* traveled throughout the Caribbean, often venturing beyond her home port in Aruba and the other islands of the Netherlands Antilles. In a bold move that I suspect was mainly for PR purposes, the *Freewinds* spent a couple of weeks in Ensenada, Mexico. Scientologists in Southern California and elsewhere in the state were urged to spend some time on the ship, or at least to come for a one day visit. Susie decided to go.

It would be a short trip, and wouldn't incur any huge expense as long as Susie didn't sign up for a course. But with Church registrars, you never know. It was a typical Scientology PR spectacle designed to give the Church some positive publicity.

Susie missed her Scientologist friends in L.A., and this was a perfect opportunity to see some of them. She drove to L.A. and stayed with a friend. From the L.A. Complex they were busing Scientologists down to Ensenada on a daily basis. It was an opportunity for a lot of West Coast Scientologists to get a look at the *Freewinds*. Other than the grueling bus ride, from L.A. to Ensenada, Susie had a good time.

As time passed, our involvement in Scientology waned. Living in Monterey was a part of the reason, but our financial condition was a big part too. We'd sold our house in L.A., and I'd sold my business assets. We also didn't have much money on account at any of the orgs. The reservoir had dwindled to a puddle.

I'd get occasional phone calls from Church staff promoting various things but I really didn't have the money to pay for more services. They'd ask me, "What are you planning to do so you can get your 'so-and-so' paid for?" I honestly didn't know, and I said so. Not a good answer when talking to Church staff. The generally accepted answer to that kind of question was supposed to go something like this: "I'm applying the Ethics Conditions and I've written up a personal program to boost my finances into affluence, and if a couple of these deals come through, I should be sitting in clover pretty soon, at which point I'll be sending you a check."

Well, that wasn't my situation, and I'd gotten tired of playing those kinds of phony games. I was rethinking the way I wanted to deal with the Church. Maybe I should be as straightforward as possible. Maybe I shouldn't be wasting time defending my situations when they seemed to conflict with what the Church wanted. I had neither the desire nor intention of getting into endless arguments with staff who weren't prepared to take no for an answer.

I got a call from someone from the Flag Liaison Office in San Mateo. He asked me, "When are you planning to start OT VII?" I said I didn't know. The caller asked if I had a plan, a program, or if I had set a target date for arriving. I said no. It was a simple answer, and it was also the truth. But that kind of answer never satisfies the Church. He then asked, "What has to happen in order for you to arrive at Flag?" Again, I didn't know. I explained that I needed something like 20 to 30 thousand dollars for set-ups, preps, eligibility etc., in order to get started. I didn't have that kind of money, and I hadn't the faintest idea how I might come up with it.

The Flag rep took a new angle. He asked, "How long do you think it'll be before you come to Flag?" What could I say? "I don't know" was the answer again. I was beginning to like my new approach. It was simple, honest and stress free—for me anyway—the caller was getting a little exasperated. He asked, "Are we talking six months, a year, two years, or what?"

I wasn't going out of my way to be obtuse. I simply didn't know. I tried to strengthen my position with logic. I said, "I don't have enough factual data to make a reliable prediction. I can say six months, I can say a year, but both would be wild guesses." Now I was starting to get exasperated. I said, "You tell me what answer you'd like to hear. It doesn't matter to me because any answer I give you isn't based on any real information."

When all else fails, the Church registrar can always play the "postulate" card. So this Flag rep says, "Let's postulate that you'll be arriving at Flag soon." Heck, I could do that. Why didn't he just ask for that in the first place? He could have saved us both some time.

Even though I wasn't doing any auditing or taking any courses, Church staff can still promote things like public events and seminars—stuff that didn't cost anything to do. I got plenty of phone calls. Sometimes I'd hem and haw, being as non-committal as I could. "Well if I'm free that weekend maybe I can make it." Depending on how the caller chose to interpret my equivocations, this kind of answer could be taken either as a yes or a no.

In Scientology, any time there's a big event, attendance is of primary importance. Event callers are at all times looking for "confirms," and usually have a daily or weekly quota for the number of people they're supposed to get. Consequently, they don't like your response to be "No, I don't think I'm going to attend." If you try to suggest that you're probably not coming to an event, org staff will always try to hard-sell you in some way, usually asking something unimaginative like, "Why not?" "I don't know" is an unacceptable response.

A Scientologist has a few options when dealing with a persistent call-in staff member. You can come up with a convincing excuse: "My aunt is having a birthday party for her cat, and I promised that I'd come. It would absolutely break her heart if I cancelled out." Or if you're not that creative, you can lie and say that you're coming, and then just not attend. (It's a common practice among Scientologists, believe me.) Or you can try to talk your way out of it by convincing the caller that your life is so full of commitments that you can't possibly attend. Sometimes this approach works, but it can be time consuming. The caller might try to suggest various solutions to your time management problems so that you can attend the event anyway. And it also invites the possibility that the event caller will go into a sales pitch about some course that will allow you to better organize your life so that you have the time to attend Scientology events.

I always tried to give the caller a qualified maybe. It didn't sound as bad as "no" and left open the hope that perhaps I was indeed going to come to the event: "Well, if I can finish up on this important project I'm working on, then I'll come. Can't make any promises, but I'll definitely try to make it." Not as blatant as an out-and-out lie but practically the same thing.

Although I'd become less involved in Church activities, there were still opportunities to stay involved. I volunteered to work with the San Jose office of the Citizens Commission on Human Rights, an activist group run by Scientologists, dedicated to the elimination of psychiatric abuse. CCHR vehemently opposes such practices as drugging, electro-shock, and involuntary treatment.

The most difficult part of getting out any Scientology related publication is getting the "Issue Authority" to publish it. I went through the procedure many times as the Director of Promotion and Marketing at Westwood Mission. But now I was donating my time and was less willing to run through bureaucratic hoops.

Sometimes you can really get the runaround. The trick is finding the most direct route to the exact person who has the authority to approve your request. That route varies depending on the content of the publication and the organization you represent. It can take over a week of phone calls and inquiries. Then if your publication doesn't comply with all Church requirements, you have to revise the disqualified material and resubmit the whole thing all over again.

Trademarks and copyrights must be properly displayed. L. Ron Hubbard excerpts must be properly referenced. Then somewhere in your publication you need to insert a very thorough legal notice. Currently, you will find something like this in all Scientology magazines, brochures, and other Church material:

In addition to the words "Scientology" and "Dianetics," the Church has also trademarked and copyrighted a number of other things. Terms like *LRH, Flag, Clear, OT,* and *Saint Hill* are but a few of the items of which they claim ownership. The Church has registered dozens of terms, words and logos which they claim can only be used with their permission.

Legal qualifications also extend to individual Scientologists. You must be officially certified in order apply the techniques of Scientology. You can't even call yourself a Scientologist without permission from the Religious Technology Center, the official sanctioning body of the Church. It's since occurred to me that the most powerful people in Scientology might be lawyers.

I knew how vigilantly the Church of Scientology guarded its copyrights. And I was familiar with the Church's penchant for aggressive legal action to prevent illicit use of their material. Since the schism of 1982, the Church was often embroiled in legal battles with ex-Scientologists who tried to operate as independent practitioners outside the Church's legalistic structure. One of the important functions of the Office of Special Affairs is to shut down such activities.

In 1996, OSA called upon a handful of us Monterey Scientologists to help them conduct a sting operation against an independent practitioner they suspected of using an unauthorized E-meter. The Church claims patent rights to this device, and tries to prevent unauthorized construction of similar devices they consider to be an infringement of their patent.

The offender in question had a counseling practice in the San Francisco area with a substantial clientele throughout California. Our job was to get him to come to our area to demonstrate his techniques, along with his "device," with the idea that we'd be able to provide OSA with ample evidence to prosecute or sue the counselor. One of our local Scientologists contacted the guy and persuaded him to come to her home in Seaside, just north of Monterey. She convinced him that she had a group of eager prospects interested in finding out about his counseling methods.

He showed up and we got a full demonstration of something he described as a variation of a biofeedback device. It used hand-held cans just like a Scientology E-meter, but beyond that, I have no idea if it had anything else in common. As best as I could tell, we pulled off the caper successfully, though I don't know what followed with OSA's investigation. I quickly forgot the whole affair.

Sometime afterward, I found myself in another clandestine OSA operation. In the mid 1990's, the internet had become a serious area of contention for the Church. A proliferation of Scientology material, especially confidential material, was appearing on the web. Also, newsgroups and internet forums were popping up everywhere, expressing harsh criticism of Scientology. The Church saw it as a major threat, and I was pressed into service to fight its latest war: the war in cyberspace.

OSA had been monitoring a few online newsgroups critical of Scientology. Their plan was to "hack" into some of these groups and cancel the most offensive messages. I suspected that the Church was most concerned with deleting the confidential OT materials that were appearing more and more on the web. Although the process of deleting others' messages seemed illegal, I was assured that it wasn't. The OSA exec I was working with told me that although it did violate accepted protocol, it was not illegal. It was just impolite. OK, if you say so.

My part in this high-tech caper wasn't much. OSA only needed me as a "front" to set up a personal internet account with a service provider. It worked this way: An OSA staff member or volunteer would log on to a newsgroup and start canceling messages. Eventually someone would lodge a complaint and the service provider would cancel that account. OSA would then set up a new account and continue the process. In order to avoid suspicion, each new account had to be initiated by a different person. Apparently OSA had recruited a number of volunteers like me to set up accounts that would usually only last a few days until the service provider got wise to the shenanigans.

I started an Internet account and conducted the whole transaction over the telephone using a credit card. Then I gave the OSA exec my log-in name and password, and they took it from there. I sent OSA a copy of the credit card receipt and got reimbursed. That was pretty much the end of it. That is until I got a letter from some law office representing the service provider from which I had set up my account.

I wasn't aware of the extent of the legal battle that the Church of Scientology was waging. I hadn't known that the Church was trying to hold internet service providers liable for copyright violations allegedly committed by their customers. The whole thing was being hashed out in the courts, and these lawyers were asking me to provide them with information regarding my account. I wasn't sure whether or not I should cooperate.

I called the OSA exec and asked what would be the best thing to do. She said that I shouldn't assist them in any way because the Church had a lawsuit in progress against the company that had contacted me. I said that was fine, I'd take care of it. I hadn't been served with a subpoena, so I wasn't under any obligation to give them information. I wrote back to the law office and informed them that I considered any transactions between myself and my service provider to be a private matter between me and the company. And so ended my brief foray into the war between Scientology and the internet.

From 1994 to 1997 my Church activities were getting fewer and further between. There were the occasional phone calls, and the get-togethers with local Scientologists. But neither Susie nor I had done any auditing and training in that span of time. The one exception was a correspondence course on the subject of art that Susie took under the supervision of the Church in San Jose. She thought it was lightweight and lacked useful information. Dissatisfied, she didn't even finish the course—a cardinal sin if you're a Scientologist. Oddly, it didn't create much of a flap. But then it was only a correspondence course costing something like fifty dollars. I suspect that had the same thing occurred on the premises of the San Jose org, it would have become a much bigger problem.

As we became less involved in Church activities we got more involved in local community activities, mostly with the schools our kids went to. Susie helped teach an art course at the elementary school, and later became the treasurer of the marching band boosters club at Monterey High School. Our son had gotten into football and track, and I became a two-sport parent booster. I designed and produced the Monterey High football program for three consecutive years.

Both Susie and I became volunteers at the Laguna Seca race track during the various races throughout the year. As volunteer workers we raised a lot of money for the high school. Our community involvement was satisfying and we thought the time we put into it was well spent.

Susie and I were undergoing a subtle transformation, one I don't think either of us were aware of. We were slowly turning into ordinary people. It was a stark contrast to the idealized image of the heroic Scientologist selflessly and nobly saving the world from all of its evils.

IN RETROSPECT: Scientologists would never say it in public, but most of them believe that they've become superior beings possessed with incredible abilities and perceptions far in advance of the average human. They can sometimes look upon the unenlightened non-Scientologists with arrogant condescension. Non-Scientologists are seen as backward and ignorant, without a clue as to how to solve their problems. Hubbard even coined an old English slang term "wog" which he defined as "...a common ordinary run-of-the-mill garden variety humanoid." In effect, a wog is a person of no significant consequence. Scientologists, on the other hand, see themselves as the most important and valuable people on Earth.

Susie and I were getting along fabulously with the unwashed masses of the "wog" world. But this sort of immersion into the common fabric of society is sometimes looked upon by the Church with caution. In fact, Scientologists consider the social status of "middle class" as suspect. That attitude is merely a reflection of Hubbard's own disdainful view of the middle class. In a Bulletin dated 16 April 1982, Hubbard stated, "...persons of the middle class...frown very terribly on anything that the least bit tries to make a better world." And he observed, "...the dull middle-class world is a sort of slavery and suicide."

No doubt in the eyes of some of our Scientologist peers, Susie and I were descending into an unsavory realm: a vulgar world that would surely corrupt us into miserable bourgeois dullards. Much to the contrary, we were enjoying productive lives, we were a credit to our community, and we were healthy and happy. I can't imagine anyone, even the most zealous Scientologist, not wanting any of that. ■

As Susie and I continued to assimilate into non-Scientology society, we started looking at our Church with greater objectivity. For example, it was getting easier to observe and acknowledge that the Church often suffered at the hands of incompetent staff. So many of them were young, inexperienced, and just not up to the task of working effectively in an organization. Many of these young staffers had little or no previous employment experience, especially the Sea Org members. They seemed naïve to the ways of the "outside" world.

Our lack of respect for certain aspects of the Church organization, didn't affect our respect for Scientology. We continued to believe that Scientology contained life's answers, and a reliable route to spiritual salvation and freedom. Even though we were living on the periphery of the Scientology world, Susie and I felt we still had a role in saving the world from destruction. It was both a duty and a responsibility. But it was also turning into a chore and a burden.

Chapter 21

Hard Sell On the High Seas

By 1998, my sphere of professional activities had expanded considerably. In addition to publishing and advertising, I had gotten into website design. Consequently, I became familiar with the internet and finding my way around the online world that was expanding daily. I'd also started becoming an active writer, though not yet published (if you don't count the one book I edited a couple of years before). I also wrote three screenplays, two which nearly reached production.

The world of politics had become a new area for me as well. Over the years, my dad had been politically active. As a prominent businessman, he'd made a few contacts and acquaintances in the California legislature. In the eighties he co-authored and helped sponsor a state ballot initiative meant to deal with lawsuit abuse.

Later, he achieved some local notoriety when he ran his dog Ernest for Congress. It was more than just a joke. He'd hoped it would draw attention towards a political process he believed had bogged down in voter apathy, and partisan infighting. As a spin-off of that campaign, we put together the Friends of Ernest organization to promote public interest in our government systems. I started writing political essays for our periodical newsletter.

Two years had passed since Susie had done any major Scientology services, and I had done nothing since we left L.A. When you're a Scientologist who's advanced as far as we had, your lack of progress will come under scrutiny. In the Church's view, a Scientologist who isn't continuing his auditing and training is manifesting some sort of problem that's impeding his progress. This problem of course can be remedied. As I've said, the remedy is always more Scientology.

The Flagship Organization started a new service available only on the *Freewinds* (also known as "The Ship"). It was called the "OT Tech Debug Service," meant for OTs who had gotten stalled on their Scientology progress. Our FSM Barry suggested that I should do it. Although I wasn't convinced the Debug Service was the answer, I was considering doing some kind of training course aboard the *Freewinds*. I thought at the very least I should be doing something rather than nothing. Besides, I believed that doing an OT training course geared specifically and exclusively for OTs would give me some kind of a boost in ability.

As it turned out, we had some leftover money on account for room and board. All I needed was the additional $750 for the OT training course I wanted to do, and a few hundred bucks for plane fare. All in all, it seemed like an inexpensive proposition, and opportunity: A week on the *Freewinds*, where the most advanced Scientologists go to do the most advanced Scientology services.

After a long series of plane connections, from San Jose, through Houston and Miami and then to Puerto Rico, I arrived in Castries, St. Lucia, a sovereign island country that's part of the Lesser Antilles. Another Scientologist (from Puerto Rico) and I waited at the airport for a *Freewinds* staff to drive us to wherever the ship was docked. I'd never been on any kind of ocean cruise before, so I was pretty excited.

As I walked up the gangway, I was met by the Quartermaster, a young, no-nonsense sort of guy who performed his duties like a sentry officer on a military base. He asked me a series of questions, the implications of which I fully understood. It was a cursory security check to make sure I wasn't a potential threat to the safety of the ship. As is the case with other orgs that deal in confidential upper level material, the Ship has its security procedures, maybe the strictest in Scientology.

My plan was to take the "Anatomy of Cause" course which was made up mostly of a particular series of taped lectures Hubbard had given back in the fifties. But before I got a chance to sign up for the course (and pay for it) I was routed to the Hubbard Guidance Center, the department that handles all of the auditing services. I hadn't arrived for auditing, so there was no need to check in to the HGC. It seemed unusual. Nevertheless, I got a Director of Processing interview and was asked to fill out an OCA personality test just as if I were getting set up to receive some auditing.

Meanwhile, I was in the process of routing onto my OT course. I'd been on the course less than a day when I was called back into the HGC. The D of P had the results of my personality test. She had a grave expression on her face as she presented the results. The graph was in a high and acceptable range in all of the categories except one. This was cause for concern; it was evidence that I needed to do the OT Tech De-Bug. I was far from convinced. Over my reservations, they insisted on sending me to see the registrar.

■ **BACKGROUND:** The OT Tech De-Bug rundown is based on the premise that there's only one reason why a Scientologist doesn't continue to make progress up the Bridge: His own reactive mind is somehow preventing him from doing so. In other words, it was my own aberrations that were keeping me from dealing with my aberrations. This sort of circular reasoning provides the rationale for much that takes place in Scientology. ■

The purpose of my visit to the HGC was becoming evident. The Flag Ship Organization intended from the start that I do the OT Tech De-Bug rundown. When I arrived at the registrar's office, the registrar looked as grave as the Director of Processing did. My entire spiritual future was at stake, and he made sure I understood that. He showed me some Hubbard references he believed substantiated his case. I got the usual spiel on the absolute necessity of continuing up the Bridge, especially when you're on the OT levels.

It took almost an hour, but he did convince me. Now I had to convince Susie. Our telephone conversation was one we'd been through many times: How do we minimize the effect of going deeper into debt?

Our Scientology expenditures had created a multiple selection of credit cards which we relied on constantly to finance our Church donations. So once again, plastic would be the payment of choice. Susie advised me which of our cards had enough available credit. Another debt, another Church service paid in full.

■ **IN RETROSPECT:** In plain terms, I was set up. I'd been blindsided by the whole sequence of events. Even my FSM Barry confided to Susie following the incident that this had been their intention: Insist that I do the De-bug program whether I wanted to or not.

I'd grown so used to this bait-and-switch tactic that it seemed reasonably normal. Naturally, I'd have to pay for the Debug service. I hadn't planned on that. I'd also have to pay for additional room and board for the extra time I'd be on the ship. But I trusted the staff to look after my best interests. I knew my treatment on the *Freewinds* had been a little underhanded, but I believed it was for my own good. ■

In addition to undergoing auditing and training, Scientologists on the Ship are expected to participate in activities on shore. It's a unique requirement found nowhere else in Scientology. I was told that interacting with the locals and taking part in outdoor recreation was part of the OT experience. The implication was that it was therapeutic.

There was another implication that I suspected was at least as important, if not more so. As the elite class of Scientologists, we were considered ambassadors for Scientology. By maintaining good relations with the local populations (not to mention contributing to their economies), we were presenting the Church of Scientology in a positive light. In Scientology lingo it's called "safe pointing."

So in addition to the auditing and training I did, I also had a good time romping about the Caribbean Islands. The *Freewinds* experience was a combination of a religious retreat, a health spa, and a vacation cruise. I particularly enjoyed meeting other Scientologists who came from all over the U.S. as well as from around the world. I made friends with a young Scientologist from Denmark who shared my taste for cigars. They sold some good name brands at the canteen, and my Danish friend and I enjoyed an evening smoke on deck while watching the ocean waves rushing past.

The additional expenses I'd incurred were relatively minor when compared to my previous Church costs. The most affluent Scientologists are constantly being hit up for donations to fund Church activities and projects. Knowing this, I'd only brought two credit cards with me; one to cover incidental expenses; the other to cover plane fare. There was only so much money a registrar could squeeze out of me.

Well, I was wrong. Again. The IAS had its own office aboard the Ship and their staff members were the most intense fund-raisers I'd ever encountered. Inevitably, I had a personal meeting with an IAS representative. She was formerly the head of the IAS in the United States and was still part of the highest level of Church executives. She seemed very nice.

We had a friendly conversation about my activities as a Scientologist and as a professional person. She was sizing me up, getting a feel for my level of loyalty and dedication to Scientology. She also needed to get a general idea of my financial standing.

I explained my credit card situation. If an IAS representative is convinced that they're not going to be able to extract a few thousand dollars out of you (and it's always the first thing they try), they'll readjust their sites and go for a secondary target. The IAS reg told me that she was trying to get a minimum $500 contribution from every Scientologist on the ship. I said that I might be willing to go that far, but my credit cards were back in my cabin. It was a stalling tactic on my part, and a lame one at that.

The reg said I could go get my credit cards and come back. Not only did she send me back to my cabin, she actually assigned an IAS staff member to escort me back to my room to ensure that I'd return. IAS Registrars have no shame and a lot of gall.

Back at the IAS office I was still resistant. I mentioned the credit limit on my cards. Not a problem. The IAS knows backwards and forwards all of the ins and outs of the credit card process. The reg asked me for the name and type of credit cards I had and then made a phone call. She had the system wired. She pressed a few phone buttons and handed the phone to me.

I was connected to the central data bank set up by my credit card company, an automated prerecorded touch-tone system. I punched in my credit card number and got a recording informing me of my current balance. I'd be able to debit the $500 without exceeding my limit, and still leave enough of a buffer for plane fare and a few expenses that might come up.

The IAS got their $500, and I'd gotten another lesson in IAS tenacity. Oddly, I felt pretty good about my donation afterwards. Why? Was it because I believed I had done something good for humanity? Maybe I felt the relief a store owner feels when the mob collects their protection money and then leaves the premises without breaking up the place.

■ **IN RETROSPECT:** Placating the IAS is impossible. Their system keeps Scientologists locked into a never ending cycle of donations. Once you give them money, you're admitting you have sufficient resources to continue giving them more money later. My donation on the Ship would hardly exempt me from later demands. It never does. ■

One evening, a dozen or so Scientologists and I were summoned to the IAS office. We were told we'd be attending a "closed door briefing," which I guess was supposed to make us feel important and special. It made me feel nervous, because I knew what was coming. This was going to be a ten-round slugfest—a brutal battle for our wallets, pocketbooks, and credit cards.

The IAS registrar who was deployed for the meeting must have been a big player within the Church hierarchy. I figured they sent in one of their heavy hitters to pull it off. I have no idea who the guy was—I'd never seen or heard of him before—and I don't know if he was a public Scientologist or part of the Sea Org. In any case, for the next hour I was subjected to a surreal experience.

It started out predictably enough. The standard material: "The Church is up against evil forces dedicated to destroying the Church. They want to destroy us because we, the Scientologists, are the ones standing in their way of achieving a slave-like domination of the entire world. Our only hope was to continue donating huge amounts of money, to the IAS."

I don't recall whether or not this guy was making a compelling case for anyone in the room or not. I wasn't paying close attention. I was caught up in my own thoughts, planning moves in advance like a chess player, figuring out the best way to get out of the room financially intact.

His patter and delivery came across as a combination of an infomercial salesman and a Sunday evening TV evangelist. Early in his sales pitch he offered to anyone who donated a minimum of five thousand dollars an exclusive publication he'd written that contained a number of money-making secrets guaranteed to increase your income. The presentation seemed cheesy, like a bad cable TV shopping program. The only thing missing were the bonus steak knives.

One of the effective aspects of group solicitations is that the registrar can take advantage of peer pressure. None of us wanted to look like we were turning our backs on the Church. And we didn't want to come off as materialistic cheapskates concerned only with our bank statements. We were, after all, loyal and dedicated Scientologists contributing to the good of the world.

The IAS reg cranked his sales routine into full gear. "Who's going to give me ten thousand dollars? Who wants to be first? Raise your hand." Despite our supposedly good and noble natures, no one at the table stepped forward.

The reg then laid his cards on the table. "I need to get five thousand dollars from everyone here tonight. The IAS needs $180,000, and we have to have it within twenty four hours. Who wants to start?" The session seemed to combine a livestock auction and a POW interrogation. We were all holding on to money that we weren't talking about, and it was time to confess and give it up. I sensed no one would be leaving the room until we coughed up some serious bucks.

The Reg started singling people out and asking them directly how much they were planning to donate. That got some hemming and hawing, but no donation pledges. Finally, one Scientologist stood up and said, "I realize how incredibly important this is. So I'm giving the IAS $12,000. I really can't afford it, and it's going to totally screw up my finances. But it's got to be done."

This is exactly the sort of thing the IAS registrar was trying to inspire in all of us. Unfortunately, no one else responded. The reg paced around the table trying to drum up more enthusiasm. Then he stopped and shifted gears. "I need to let you in on something. There's a spaceship outside, not too far from here, and it's going to be leaving pretty soon. Anyone who's interested, we can all get on board."

For a moment I believed that he believed it. For a moment I even believed it. For a moment I believed that we had all lost our minds. No one said anything. Perhaps it was best not to disturb a lunatic in the middle of a delusional tirade. I couldn't tell if he was just trying to tell a weird joke to put us at ease, or if he was actually nuts.

After a pause, someone spoke up. "So, uh, what does this spaceship look like?" I'd had enough. Before the reg had a chance to answer, I said, "It's about the color of this purple hat sitting on the table." The Freewinds IAS lady I'd first met was sitting next to me. She said quietly and calmly, "Thank you," and I got the impression that she too thought our session had gone over the top.

Just when I thought things couldn't get any more unreal, the IAS reg walked up behind me and whispered in my ear, "Can I get $500 from you?" I didn't know how to respond. Was I supposed to answer out loud, or was this some kind of confidential exchange exclusively between the two of us?" He came up to me a couple more times and did the same thing. "Just $500 dollars."

I finally whispered back, "Can't do it, don't have it." My mind was a jumble of confusion. How am I going to get out of this? I knew the answer to that, and it was going to cost me. I made an offer: "The best I can do is $250. You can take it out of one of my credit cards. That's it, take it or leave it." He took it. No one ever said that saving the planet was going to be cheap.

Chapter 22

Second Thoughts

Despite my financial misadventures aboard the *Freewinds*, I felt I was getting positive gains. I took what I learned and found ways to apply it to situations in everyday life. And I think it's always a healthy exercise to occasionally take stock of one's life and determine where you're at and where you want to be. I frequently used Scientology to help me plot out workable plans towards personal goals. The future seemed bright.

I'd completed my course, and had finished the rundown, so it was time to route out of the Flagship Org, and head for home. That meant following the procedures as specified by Hubbard. One such directive is something called the "re-sign" policy[1] (as in signing up again). Hubbard states, "The re-sign line is also very key to an organization's prosperity. It brings further income, and proves conclusively that the last service received by the public person was of high quality." The bottom line to this policy is, "every completion gets routed to the reg."

I'd attested to the completion of my services, so I was routed back to the registrar's office. It's expected that every Scientologist should be ready to sign up for their next service. In the event that this doesn't happen, the reg can send the completion back to the Qualifications Division to ensure that there hasn't been anything missed in the auditing or training. In the Church's view, anyone who isn't ready to enthusiastically sign up for their next service must not have gotten everything possible out of what they just completed.

There I was again, sitting at the registrar's desk. I explained to him I'd been financially drained by the IAS. I told him I'd made a firm decision that I wasn't going to spend any more money on Scientology until I'd gotten my debts under control. The reg was understanding, but only to a point. He grabbed one of his volumes of Hubbard policy letters, and opened to the applicable page. He handed it to me and said, "Per this policy I have to ensure that we haven't missed anything technically."

I'd been in this situation dozens of times, and found that different registrars enforced this policy in varying degrees of strictness. Although this particular reg made it clear that he might be obligated to send me back to Qual, he did offer me a compromise: If I were to put down some kind of advance payment for—say, another course—this would sufficiently demonstrate my willingness to continue my training aboard the Ship.

It seemed like a two-bit shakedown. I felt like a traveler forced to bribe a customs agent in order to leave a Third World country. I decided it was time to draw the line. I didn't have to cough up another couple hundred bucks to show some registrar I was a legitimate service completion.

This was no longer about Hubbard policy or Church procedure. It was about maintaining my integrity. I wasn't going to be cowed into racking up more debt on my credit cards just to avoid getting routed back to the Qualifications Office. I was certain of the gains I'd gotten, and if they wanted to challenge that, so be it.

The registrar sent me back to Qual with the indifferent brusqueness of a minor bureaucrat. It reminded me of my last visit to the Department of Motor Vehicles. Although I thought I was being jerked around, I smiled and played along. Sometimes policy is policy, rules are rules, and I knew when to keep my mouth shut. If I was going to get off the *Freewinds* with my good standing intact, I'd have to be diplomatic.

I forgot one factor. Once I completed my service, I'd become low priority public for every staff member of the Flagship Organization. Completing the routing form that would give me authorization to leave the Ship would contribute no production statistics for anyone. Consequently, I had a hard time finding the Qualifications Examiner, and she was in no great hurry to find me. To add to that, it was Thursday morning, and all staff were rushing to get their stats up by the 2:00 PM deadline.

I went back to my room and kicked back. No one would be looking for me or demanding my time, or trying to extract more money out of me. And I had time to reflect on my stay on the Ship. I felt that in the span of fifteen days I'd jammed in a month's worth of activity. There were good times, tough times, and a few frustrating times. Par for the course for any Scientologist.

My worries weren't over: What if I was ordered to do some corrective auditing or training? The Qual Division would charge me by the hour for correcting anything missed on my study course. And I'd have to pay for more auditing to repair my De-bug. I could hardly face the prospect of another week on the ship. But it was within the realm of possibilities.

Maybe I'd just leave the ship, take a cab to the nearest airport and head for home. But they were holding my passport. Would they relinquish it to me if I were to leave in such an unauthorized fashion? There was a good chance they wouldn't. Even if they did, my status as a Scientologist would be in serious trouble. Sooner or later, I'd have to come back to the Ship or maybe to Flag, and "handle my blow." If I refused to cooperate, I'd eventually get expelled.

There was a better solution. I just had to convince the Examiner I thoroughly loved the Tech Debug Rundown. And I'd have to do it all on an E-meter. I was going to have to be as clean as Simon Pure.

It was late in the afternoon when I finally got an appointment with the Examiner. If there was ever such a thing as a big Scientology happy face, I figured I'd better come up with one now. If I exhibited any sign that my auditing and training were less than perfect, I'd need to go back in session or restudy, all at my expense.

I picked up the E-meter cans, and I was asked if anything had been missed during my recent auditing or during the course I'd finished. Nothing read on the meter, and I was out of there. What a relief. I felt like I beat the system. I stood up to the registrar, refusing to give him a cent, and got off scot-free. On the other hand, I could have avoided a trip to Qual had I bought off the registrar with a $200 advance payment towards my next course. Each additional day of room and board cost me $250. No matter how you play it, the Church always gets their piece of the action. In any case, I was anxious to get back home. I had lots of things I wanted to do. I felt like a prisoner who'd just been paroled.

In order for my Debug service to be officially complete, I now had to start my next course—that is unless I wanted to be ordered back to the ship to re-do the whole thing. I called the San Jose Org and signed up for the Student Hat Course. I'd done it years ago, but procedures had changed. There was now something called the "Golden Age of Tech," a new study procedure which meant that I'd have to re-do the course using what was supposedly a new system of instruction and testing.

The org in San Jose was about eighty miles from Monterey, a long commute. My mom lived in San Jose, so I stayed with her and did the course full-time, day and night. I slugged my way through the course and finished in four days.

Scientology had become a chore for me. But I felt duty bound to continue. I still believed Scientology was benefiting me, even though the experience wasn't always pleasant.

Throughout 1999, Susie was getting a lot of calls from Flag and the Flagship Org. There was a big push for OTs to retrain and re-audit on their levels using the new Golden Age of Tech procedures. The GAT was promoted as a revolutionary approach to studying Scientology that claimed to achieve technical perfection.

The new procedures required Scientologists to redo certain parts of their previous auditing and training in order to keep their certificates valid. Although Susie had already completed OT VIII, she was supposed to go through the OT VII and VIII again, using the revised "study tech." It seemed unnecessary to me. I'd done the GAT method on the Freewinds and at the San Jose org, and I wasn't very impressed. It seemed that Scientology study had gotten rote and robotic.

In 2000, Susie went back to Flag even though she didn't have the money to pay for redoing any of her auditing and training. She was coaxed into returning to Clearwater so she could read a confidential bulletin by Hubbard. Supposedly, by merely reading the bulletin, a significant revelation would result and consequently remove any stops impeding her progress on the Bridge.

What actually happened was very different, and took us both by surprise. When Susie returned from Flag, her first comment was, "It didn't go very well, and I'm not happy about it." She'd done a standard Director of Processing interview, which was given to the Senior Case Supervisor to look over. The Senior CS then designated Susie an "illegal PC," and therefore not eligible to view the confidential bulletin.

This was a replay of our situation in 1986. Back then, we'd successfully petitioned the Church to reinstate our status. Now the Senior C/S at Flag decided to revoke that status without an explanation other than it was in compliance with applicable policy. Flag had dragged her all the way to Clearwater for that? Susie was understandably upset.

I was enraged.

Susie's sister still worked for the FBI and the Church was still wary of Scientologists with family connections to government agencies. And covert infiltration was still one of the Church's biggest fears. For reasons unknown to us, Susie was once again viewed as a security risk.

Susie submitted a petition like she did in 1986, to the Office of the Senior Case Supervisor International. It was refused with no reason given. Her petition rejection seemed so swift and final that I didn't even try to submit one. Until further notice, neither of us would be eligible for any Scientology auditing.

So here we were, quasi-Scientologists, half in and half out. Although we'd been disbarred from auditing, the "illegal PC" didn't prevent us from doing training. The Flag Ethics Officer put together an "ethics program," of training courses for Susie. She was less than enthusiastic. We knew that no official procedure existed for our situation other than petitioning the Church. And that had been turned down. As long as Susie's sister remained in the FBI our status would probably stay the same. Even so, that wasn't the real reason that the Ethics Officer wanted Susie to continue her training. As a Scientologist, and especially as an OT, she was expected to continue doing services in spite of her reduced status.

I got the same sort of prodding from the San Jose org. I'd get calls from time to time from a registrar urging me to get started on a course. But I wasn't very interested. I felt a little

223

estranged, and didn't feel very motivated. And I knew that Scientology training wouldn't change my status. In the eyes of the Church, I was a potential security risk, and that was that. Never mind that there was never any specific evidence other than that my sister-in-law worked for the FBI.

Maybe the Church knew something about our government connections that I didn't know. Or maybe it was just a case of the Church mindlessly complying with Hubbard policy without taking into account the specific circumstances of the situation. Susie and I speculated that if we were to show up at Flag with a check for $100,000 ready to sign up for all the auditing we could possibly do, our eligibility status would have been resolved in no time.

Because we didn't have that kind of money, Susie and I were becoming low priority Scientologists with little leverage. Who'd go to bat for us when there was no percentage in it? We didn't talk about it much, but both of us were simmering in a stew of resentment.

Meanwhile real life was in full progress. Our son graduated from high school and was attending college. Our daughter was in high school and I was helping her learn to drive. Susie was elected treasurer of the high school band boosters club, and when she wasn't keeping the books for my business, she remained active in school events. I'd discovered community theater, and began performing in musicals at the Monterey junior college.

In 1999, my dad formed the Friends of Ernest Political Action Committee to put together a ballot initiative for the March 2000 election. It was named for Ernest, the same dog he ran for Congress in 1996. The initiative eventually became California Proposition 23, or the "None of the Above Ballot Initiative." I appointed myself FOEPAC Director of Special

Affairs, a little private joke with myself, giving a subtle nod to the Church of Scientology's Office of Special Affairs.

Prop. 23 would add a "none of the above" choice for federal and state candidate elections. Our initiative was modeled after a Nevada statute which has had a "none of the above" ballot option since 1976. I handled campaign promotion including a "None of the Above" website. I also dealt with media inquiries. Politics was a whole new game for me, and I was learning it as I went along. In the end, the initiative didn't pass, but it sparked my interest in political issues.

Then in late 2000 I came up with an idea for my fledgling political organization. I put together a proposal for Friends of Ernest to sponsor a local radio show that would reflect our organization's spirit and purpose. I'd be the host, and be responsible for the material and format. It was kind of a crazy idea, considering I'd never done anything like it before. But I thought I was a good public speaker. It was at least worth a try and I was confident I could write, record, and produce our radio commercials.

In January 2001, I launched *Uncommon Sense*, a weekly, two-hour radio show every Sunday, on KSCO, a Santa Cruz talk-radio station which broadcast throughout the Monterey Bay area and Salinas. It was a call-in talk show driven by current topics and events in the news. I hoped I could provide an unconventional and fresh perspective on the popular subjects of the day.

In the beginning I was a little rough around the edges. It took a while for me to develop a professional broadcast delivery, but I made up for my shortcomings with thorough preparation. I showed up every week with a wealth of material, all documented from credible sources. I thought I expressed my opinions with an articulate wit, and I had a good rapport with the listeners. The show achieved some modest success, no mean feat for Sunday radio.

I was becoming somewhat of a small-town political pundit and journalist, and in a small way, a member of the local media. The irony of that hadn't escaped me. I knew how much Hubbard and the Church of Scientology distrusted the news media. In fact, the Hubbard Policy Letter that had designated me an illegal PC also specified that members of the news media were subject to this policy as well.

I had no great love for the media establishment. In many ways I thought the Church's disdain for the press was justified. But as I got more involved, I realized you couldn't paint the news with a universally broad brush. While I criticized the media constantly on my own show, I recognized that it was possible to get factual and credible information too. I also discovered that if you took the time to investigate, you could get to the real facts behind questionable or dubious reports.

For years I'd experienced things in the Church I disagreed with. At times there were facts (or the lack thereof) that didn't add up to my satisfaction. I'd viewed these as the minor glitches one encountered in any large organization. But now I was questioning my current relationship with Scientology. Was it a good one? A bad one? And how did the Church view its relationship with me?

Was I really such a potential liability? I hadn't done anything to damage any orgs, but the "Illegal PCs" policy letter implied that I might be so inclined. I was beginning to have serious doubts about my relationship with the Church. Did I want to continue being a Scientologist forbidden to move up the Bridge, or did I want to be something else? And if so, what?

I didn't know.

I don't recall the exact day or precise moment it happened, but I began looking at Scientology a little differently. Everything I knew and understood about the Church came exclusively from Scientology sources. Anything else was suspect. But now that I was a small-time investigative journalist, I thought that my approach should be different.

If the Church of Scientology was everything it claimed to be, then they should be able to stand up to whatever scrutiny I could apply. I wouldn't have considered this approach before, and I admit it made me uneasy, as though I were about to partake in something illicit and taboo. But maybe there was a side to Scientology that I hadn't considered. Maybe Church PR had only been painting a partial picture. Maybe there was a reason the Church insisted on telling their side of the story to the exclusion of all other views. Maybe there were things the Church of Scientology would prefer its members not know.

Chapter 23

Push Comes To Shove

I'd gotten pretty good at searching the internet for news and information, and the web had become an essential resource. Just by typing "Scientology" into any search engine, I'd get dozens of links to all sorts of websites. However, as an "investigative journalist," I took a skeptical approach to my findings.

There are a lot of kooks and crackpots on the web. You can perform your own experiment to demonstrate this. Using your favorite search engine, type in the keywords, "UFO/Jesus/ Nazi," and you can watch the paranoid kaleidoscope unfold before your eyes. If that doesn't convince you, try, "IRS/Rothschild/ Rockefeller," or "U.N./World Bank/ZIP Code."

In addition to the nut cases, I discovered that there were a lot of hysterical people who loathed Scientology, which they saw as an insidious network of oppression and evil plaguing the world. I wasn't convinced of that, but I was willing to examine anything that appeared to be legitimate criticism. With some good judgment, and a little common sense I started to compile a collection of credible information.

A few things in particular caught my attention. In 1995, Scientologist Lisa McPherson died while under the care and supervision of Church staff at Flag. While undergoing an auditing program called the Introspection Rundown, Lisa had become critically ill. By the time she arrived at the hospital, she was dead. The Church called it an unfortunate accident, while others insisted it was negligence. A Florida court considered filing criminal charges, but that case never materialized. The McPherson family filed a civil suit against the Church.

In my analysis, I thought there was a good possibility that Lisa's death could have been avoided had Flag done things differently. What may have killed Lisa was an excessively strict adherence to Church policies and procedures. Church staff may have tried to deal with Lisa's condition using Scientology techniques long after medical attention was warranted. It's possible that by the time they recognized they had a medical emergency on their hands, it was too late. It may have been a deadly error in judgment.

Another factor in play would have been the single-minded pursuit of "valuable final products," which are reflected in the Church's weekly production stats. If a Scientologist were to become ill during Scientology processing, this would reflect negatively on the Technical Division. Sending a PC to the hospital after an auditing process would have been devastating.

I can recognize damage control and PR spin when I see it, and the Church of Scientology was unmistakably put on the defensive. Official Church statements from their spokespeople seemed oblivious to the tragic facts. And as usual, Church members were kept completely in the dark.

The Church did what they always do when dealing with mishaps that create PR problems: They circle the wagons and handle the situation internally. I suspect that much of what actually happened within the Church after Lisa McPherson's death will never see the light of day. It's a safe bet that some Church staff got disciplined, reprimanded, perhaps even demoted. But the public at large, not to mention public Scientologists, would never know about it.

As compelling as the McPherson story was, I wasn't ready to condemn the entire Church for the appallingly poor judgment of an incompetent few. But I wondered, where I should I draw the line? How much bad behavior would I have to discover before I had enough? Was there a limit to what I'd condone in the name of Scientology?

Day by eye-opening day, I continued my expedition through the internet. Critics of Scientology weren't hard to find. Websites, newsgroups, forums, and e-mail lists were dedicated to discrediting Hubbard, the Church, and its members. In the beginning I was put off by the hostility that so many critics had, and I didn't have an easy time wading through the vitriol.

I came across a newsgroup known as ARS (which stands for "alt religion scientology"). My first impression was that it was downright ugly. I found it difficult to take some of the ARS posters seriously. As a group they were obsessively hostile against everything concerning Scientology. I noticed that many of them were easily provoked into over-the-top rants, paranoid speculations, and contentious debates that usually went nowhere. I wanted something more credible than angry missives from people in need of a real life.

Back in the eighties, when scores of Scientologists were leaving the Church, I'd become aware of something called the "Free Zone." These were ex-members who broke away from the official Church and continued to practice the principles and techniques of Scientology on their own. Of course such people were looked upon with scorn by those of us loyal to the Church. The official party line was that these dissident Scientologists had devious agendas, and wanted to pervert Hubbard's technology and co-opt Scientology for their own sinister ends.

I discovered an active "underground" association of ex-members still studying and practicing Scientology. It was flimsily organized, composed of a number of factions and loosely knit groups. These so-called Free Zoners were carrying on with their Scientology activities in their own way. They also communicated frequently on the Internet, many maintaining their own websites.

Typically, they were ex-Sea Org members or other Church staff, who had considerable experience with Scientology technology. Some had been in high-level positions. Some had even worked directly with L. Ron Hubbard. Many were well trained auditors capable of delivering OT-level auditing. Some had become fed up with the Church; others had been kicked out.

Their accounts weren't hard to find on the internet. A number of these unorthodox Scientologists told their personal stories in impressive detail. I found something in common with many of them. We'd all been at one time or another at the short end of unreasonably rigid and sometimes mindlessly arbitrary Church policy. I found that most Free Zoners believed the Church had been so badly managed for a number of years that it was being run into the ground, and reform from within was no longer feasible.

If the allegations from the Free Zone were accurate, where did I stand? If I were to continue as a Scientologist, did I want to be a reformer? Maybe I'd become a whistleblower and crusader, fighting corruption from within. Maybe I'd become a rebellious heretic, excommunicated by the orthodox Scientology establishment. Maybe I'd just throw up my hands and walk away.

Throughout 2001 I was sorting out a lot of things involving my relationship with Scientology. I was disaffected, but I couldn't express my dissatisfaction to any Scientologist in good standing without having it reported to the Church. I didn't even tell Susie for fear of starting a flap with the Church and creating a rift between us.

The Church has an official procedure that Scientologists can use when they observe something they think needs correcting. They can write up a report and send it to the Inspections Unit of the Religious Technology Center. The RTC is responsible for ensuring the integrity of the Scientology technology, and making sure it isn't being altered, misapplied or abused. They also oversee the various official certifications that allow members to be professional auditors, and allow individuals to establish their own Missions, Churches and other Scientology groups.

I thought that writing up a report to the RTC would be a bureaucratic ritual that would accomplish nothing. Further, if I were to actually write up my findings, I'd have to acknowledge I was privy to subversive information from forbidden sources. If I submitted a report, the RTC would start investigating me! I was heading down a path from which I might not be able to return. My good standing as a Church member stood on very shaky ground and I faced a real possibility of expulsion.

Getting kicked out of the Church in itself didn't bother me. It was the aftermath that concerned me. If I refused to cooperate with the Church justice system, I'd eventually be declared a Suppressive Person. My fellow Scientologists, good friends and acquaintances among them, would be obligated to cease all contact with me. Would I be able to live with those consequences? There was a more serious question: How would my wife react?

In March, we got a surprise visit from the Church. I came home early that afternoon to watch the NCAA basketball tournament and found two well-dressed men in my living room talking to Susie. She introduced them and said they were from the Chaplain's Office International. They'd shown up out of the blue. They said they were on a worldwide tour visiting Scientologists who had unusual situations, predicaments, or circumstances that might not be easily addressed through normal Church channels.

One of these men wanted to do an extensive interview with Susie, to find out how she was doing, and so forth, and perhaps assist us in resolving our Illegal PC status. While it all seemed reasonable, I was a bit suspicious. I thought they might have an unstated reason for being here, especially considering how they showed up without warning.

My suspicion was more than a case of my active imagination running away with me. There was a real situation here that would be of some legitimate concern to Church management. By virtue of our illegal status, the Church had already acknowledged that we were a potential risk. Adding to that risk, Susie and I were OTs. We were reputable members, somewhat prominent and part of the upper echelon of Scientology with a full knowledge of confidential materials. If our relationship with the Church turned sour, that could create a bad PR situation.

Whenever possible, the Church tries to head off trouble before it starts. I wondered if this visit wasn't a preemptive attempt to assess our situation for evidence of possible impending trouble. That possibility already existed. I had been, after all, downloading disparaging "forbidden knowledge," about the Church. The Church of Scientology's Office of Special Affairs has an investigations division, and upper level management is routinely apprised of what's going on throughout the Church network. Were Susie and I being considered "persons of interest" in a preliminary investigation?

Susie's interview lasted a little more than an hour. After the two execs left, I asked her how it went. She seemed upbeat. It was an opportunity to express some of her feelings and concerns in regards to our lowered status. She had a chance to vent some of her frustrations and felt better for it. The interviewer said he'd look into her situation and find out if there were any options that might have gone unexplored.

We never heard from them again, nor did we ever again hear from anyone representing the Chaplain's Office International. I'd at least expected a follow up letter or phone call letting us know that our matter had been referred to some Church department or official. Susie hoped that they might find an avenue through which we could pursue a way to restore our status. Nothing happened, and it seemed suspicious to me. For all I knew there was actually no such thing as the Chaplain's Office International.

Though Susie and I were ineligible for auditing, we were still in good standing with the International Association of Scientologists. We attended a banquet in San Jose to honor the more luminary members who had donated significant sums of money. We received a plaque recognizing our dedication to the IAS. Even though we were no longer eligible for Scientology auditing, we remained valuable members as long as the IAS recognized our donation potential.

One afternoon, I got a phone call at my office from Bridgett, the IAS registrar we'd known from LA. She told me there was a new push to get donations from their IAS members. This was hardly news to me. The IAS was perpetually caught up in frantic attempts to fulfill their latest quota to meet whatever the latest threat to Scientology was.

Bridgett was short on details, but she insisted the latest IAS project was in dire need of funds, lots of it, and right now. She wanted a minimum of $5,000 from me. More than that if I could manage it. She apologized for calling me at my office, explaining she couldn't reach Susie at home. She knew I didn't ordinarily conduct Church business at work, and she also knew that any donations would have to be approved by Susie first. The problem was, it was 1:30 PM on Thursday, and she was under the gun to meet her target by the weekly deadline. I told her I wouldn't alter my household financial policy just to make her production stats look good for the week. If she wanted to pursue the matter, she'd have to get Susie's OK.

When it came to giving money to the IAS, Susie and I always made sure it was a joint agreement before writing the check or debiting a credit card. So when I finally had a chance to talk to Susie about Bridget's request, I said that we hadn't done much in Scientology as of late, and by donating $5,000 we could make a positive gesture towards supporting our Church.

I'm not sure if I believed my own reasoning. But there was a practical aspect: We'd be maintaining our good standing with the Church in light of our lowered status, and at the same time we could keep the IAS off our backs for a while. It was a weird combination of purchasing indulgences from the pre-Reformation Catholic Church and paying protection money to the mob. In any case, we decided the IAS should get their money.

In spite of my recent doubts about the Church, I held on to the belief that Scientology was the only way the world could be salvaged. I just wasn't so sure anymore if the Church as an organization would ever be able to pull it off.

As I sometimes like to say, "No good deed goes unpunished." Soon after we made our $5,000 donation. Susie began getting phone calls from the IAS L.A. office imploring her to donate more money. They reasoned that since we donated money only days before, we should be able to do it again! I was insulted and outraged.

Things started getting out of hand. Each time Susie turned down an IAS reg, she'd get a phone call a few minutes later from an exec higher up in the organization. We were beside ourselves—dumbfounded, and at a loss to understand these rude intrusions on our good nature. Was the IAS aware they were tarnishing what was until now a good relationship? They seemed clueless to the adverse effect they were creating.

I told Susie that giving the IAS money was like feeding a stray animal. Once you do it the first time, the animal keeps coming back. And like the stray cat that knows where the food is, the IAS would keep coming back.

And come back they did.

On the afternoon of September 10, 2001, I got a phone call from Susie. She sounded frantic and distressed. "I need you to come home right away. Bridgett's been here all day and I can't get rid of her. She wants another $5,000 and she won't take no for an answer."

I'd had enough of Bridgett and the whole damned IAS. I had an unwelcome guest in my home who wouldn't leave and there's no way I was going to put up with it. When I got home, Susie and Bridgett were talking in the kitchen. I felt no need to mince words. I said, "Bridgett, Susie asked me to come home and get rid of you."

Bridgett reacted surprised, but maintained a friendly demeanor. Unperturbed, she went into a long explanation of how she was on a special IAS mission from L.A. and was helping the San Jose office generate more donations. She figured as long as she was "in the area" she'd pay Susie a visit and see how things were going. I then learned that earlier in the day the two had lunch downtown. It seems that when they returned to the house, Bridgett started making her hard-sell pitch for $5,000.

I had no intention of giving Bridgett another penny. That much was certain, but I'd need patience in order to get her to leave on her own accord. I could have said, "Get out of my house, you're trespassing." But I'd have to be willing to back it up by calling the police if she refused to leave. I opted for a less dramatic solution. I'd let her go through her whole sales routine, while I listened politely. Sooner or later, she'd run out of material, and then I could inform her we weren't going to give her any money.

We sat down at our kitchen table, and I let Bridgett go through her paces. She opened up a three-inch-thick loose-leaf binder full of Hubbard references, press releases, and other material. She tried her best to convince us that it was absolutely vital that all Scientologists, right here and now, to dig deep and figure out a way to come up with money for the IAS. Her rhetoric followed the standard pattern I'd been hearing for years now. I'd gotten so used to this routine that it wasn't creating the sort of impression it used to.

A number of questions were spinning around in my mind. Had something happened recently within the Church that caused the IAS to suddenly step up their activities? And why was Bridgett investing so much time and effort (four hours and counting, plus the 150 mile round trip from the San Jose org). Was the Church of Scientology really under some terrible threat? Then I thought perhaps someone within the Church had given Bridgett and the IAS the impression that Susie and I were holding on to significant assets which they might be able to tap into.

Bridgett finished her spiel, so now it was my turn. I calmly explained that our current financial scene made any further donations impossible. Then I suggested that continuing with her presentation would be a poor use of her time, since it wasn't going to result in any money from us.

Bridgett looked confused. How could a responsible Scientologist turn away an IAS registrar in such dire need? She couldn't figure it out and I felt no obligation to explain further. All she needed to understand was that she was going to walk away without any money.

It took several hours, but it finally sunk in. I tried to soften her defeat by saying I appreciated her dedication, and that I understood her motives. "I understand that sometimes desperate times often call for desperate measures." She bristled at that, insisting that neither the times nor the measures were at all desperate. I apologized for my misstatement and cordially sent Bridgett on her way.

By now it was after six, so I dashed down to the local liquor store to get a bottle of beer. It was time to kick back and enjoy a little Monday Night Football. Around the corner I noticed a familiar car parked at the curb. It was Bridgett's. She was sitting inside talking on a cell phone. Perhaps we hadn't seen the last of her. When I returned home minutes later, the car was still there. Bridget was busy going through some papers in a folder.

As the evening progressed, I interrupted my football viewing a couple of times to go outside and see if Bridget was still parked on the roadside. She was. Although she finally left around 8:30 PM, I had a difficult time enjoying the rest of the football game, wondering if zealous Scientologists might be returning to our house. Even if they did, they weren't getting any money. I'd lost my willingness to acquiesce to the perpetual demands of the Church.

The events of that day added to my doubts and reservations about the Church. Something was seriously wrong with the organization. But who could reform it, and how would it be done? And would the effort be worth it in the end?

Chapter 24

Wake Up Call

I was still in bed when Susie rushed in from the family room to wake me up. She'd been watching the news on TV and informed me, "We've been attacked. Someone blew up the Twin Towers and the Pentagon." I jumped out of bed and turned on the radio just in time to hear about the first tower crumbling to the ground.

The shock of the sudden news threw me into a maelstrom of confusion. My mind flashed to the IAS encounter of the prior evening, mere hours ago. I was momentarily transfixed, as conspiracy theories paraded through my disoriented imagination. I couldn't help wondering if the Church knew the attacks were coming. Had they been making a last-ditch effort to raise money before the disaster? Maybe their foreknowledge had occurred on some kind of intuitive level. In those first moments it all seemed possible to me.

I wasn't at all surprised when the phone rang and it was none other than Bridget. She wailed to Susie, "It's the psychiatrists! They're the ones behind this."

So much for *my* conspiracy theories.

Bridgett's accusation wasn't out of character. Scientologists believe all of the world's problems can be traced to psychiatry. Over the years the Church has blamed psychiatry for the Nazis, Communism, the Yugoslav wars, drugs, and school violence. Now we could add international terrorism to the list. Apparently Bridgett hadn't given up on us. She insisted that now more than ever we had to donate money to the IAS. Susie got a little miffed at Bridgett's audacious appeal, but politely told her no.

■ **BACKGROUND:** The Church of Scientology has a well-deserved reputation for exploiting disasters as an appeal for donations, and as a means for getting Scientologists more active in Church activities. To the uninitiated, what might appear as taking unscrupulous advantage of the misfortunes of others is cheerfully promoted by the Church as improving conditions in society. ■

While the country began to rally together, the Church went into a maximum effort to get its members mobilized. Briefings were organized throughout the Scientology network in an attempt to impress upon Scientologists that now more than ever we had to step up our Scientology activities.

Later in the day we got a phone call from a registrar from the San Jose org. He talked to Susie about what her plans were for starting a new course. Susie said she didn't even want to think about Scientology right now, as she had more immediate concerns on her mind. She had relatives, including a sister and brother-in-law who lived in NYC. But mainly she was concerned about one uncle in particular who worked for a company that had an office at the World Trade Center. She was waiting for news from family back east.

This registrar didn't back off. He told Susie that because of the terrorist attacks, it was vitally important she start working out how she's going to get started on her next Church service. Susie was insulted, but kept her cool. She said that she needed to keep the phone line open and promised that they could talk later when things weren't in such turmoil.

The next day we got more phone calls. Scientologists all over the world were instructed to go to their local Church organization for an important briefing to be delivered by Chairman of the Board David Miscavige. Churches were urging their members to purchase and distribute a Hubbard pamphlet called "The Way to Happiness." Church members were also being asked to go to Manhattan as Volunteer Ministers to provide spiritual assistance for the firefighters and those who had suffered losses.

The Church came up with an official watchword phrase to describe the terrorist attacks. From here on out the buzzword was "wake-up call." Terrorism was being used as a call to arms meant to inspire members to promote Scientology more intensely and boost activity within all of the Church organizations.

Meanwhile, I was experiencing my own wake-up call. I'd been swept into a jumble of conflicting thoughts and emotions, trying to make sense out of something devoid of sense, trying to grasp some meaning out of the unimaginable horror of 9-11. In the midst of my confusion I stopped and asked myself, what did all of this mean to me as a Scientologist?

Like so many other Americans, my view of the world changed after September 11. My view of the Church of Scientology changed as well. As best as I can describe it, the 9-11 disaster served as a catalyst that jarred my perspective into a new point of view. I could now see the Church with an objective frame of reference and a clarity I'd never had before. My relationship with Scientology had changed in a way that couldn't be reversed.

Several days later, we received *Inspector General's Bulletin No. 44* from the Religious Technology Center[1] issued by David Miscavige titled, "Wake Up Call—The Urgency of

Planetary Clearing." It contained all the predictable stuff about the need for Scientologists, now more than ever, to do whatever it takes to move up the Scientology Bridge. It also contained one very curious claim: "Osama bin Laden—has a psychiatrist as his right-hand man."

Miscavige was referring to Ayman al-Zawahiri, a Saudi doctor known to be instrumental in the training of al-Quaeda terrorists. This was not mere speculation as far as Miscavige was concerned. He said, "This is not conjecture. It is fact."

I was pretty news-savvy, and I hadn't heard anything suggesting psychiatrists were in any way involved. On my radio show, I took pride in my fact checking. I'd spend hours during the week doing follow up research on the news and issues of the day. I decided to look into what I thought was an interesting allegation. I figured if I could confirm Miscavige's claim, it would be a great scoop for my show.

I scoured the Internet for info on al-Zawahiri, and found reports from a variety of sources. The U.S. government had an extensive rap sheet on him with detailed information on his personal history, his family, and his international connections. He was a surgeon who received his degree from the University of Cairo Faculty of Medicine. His involvement in training terrorists was well documented. But there was no evidence that he'd ever had any involvement with the psychiatric field.

By coincidence, I'd received the latest issue of *Freedom*, a magazine put out by the Church of Scientology Office of Special Affairs. The magazine covers a number of political and social issues from a Scientology perspective, and tries to present itself as a credible source of investigative journalism. In an exposé on terrorism, the Church stuck to their story: Ayman al-Zawahiri was a psychiatrist. They cited their source as "officials in the Egyptian government."

I wondered, what "officials," and what part of the "Egyptian government" was reporting this? And why, in my extensive research, was I unable to find any evidence of this? If he were a psychiatrist, wouldn't that be a matter of public record? Was *Freedom Magazine* implying that al-Zawahiri was a psychiatrist, but it was some kind of a secret that could only be revealed through unnamed sources? The whole thing looked deceptive and misleading. I concluded that the Church had fabricated the story to fit into their own anti-psychiatry propaganda.

To some degree one can justify the means towards a worthwhile end. But there's such a thing as stepping over the line. If the Church of Scientology was willing to color the facts with misleading information, what other ethical compromises were they willing to make?

In the weeks and months following 9-11, I stepped up my research on Scientology. I downloaded video clips of several Scientologists who had been recently expelled. They were OTs who had been long-time members and had gotten into hot water by questioning Church policies. When they wouldn't back down, they were expelled. Consequently, they publicly renounced their membership and alleged that the Church was suffering the ill effects of corrupt management.

It was a serious accusation and it got my attention. If the Church was being mishandled by unscrupulous executives, then the possibility of reform might be out of reach. Attempts to expose the corruption could be squelched by executives covering up their own misconduct.

Litigation always seemed to go hand in hand with Church activities. For as long as I've been a Scientologist there has been a continuous succession of lawsuits involving the Church. Now because of the Internet, volumes of court records were readily available.

I read a number of legal testimonies given by ex-Sea Org members, all telling their respective stories under oath. Their accounts contained common elements of abuse, mismanagement, and fanatical hysteria. They all painted a similar picture of the Church as extremists, bent on doing anything necessary to quell dissent within their ranks. Were these ex-members lying under oath, or telling the truth? I didn't know for sure. But the more I examined the evidence, the more credible the stories became.

Perhaps the most outrageous story I found came from two girls, Astra and Zoe Woodcraft who had spent most of their childhood in the Cadet Org, the department of the Sea Org that was responsible for the care and supervision of children belonging to the parents of Sea Org staff. Their mother was a Sea Org member who'd taken sole custody after the father, Lawrence Woodcraft, had been expelled from the Church. The children were eventually rescued by Lawrence who took them out of the Cadet Org. Once free from Church interference, the girls made a number of videos describing their experiences growing up within the Sea Org environment. The ugliness of their stories of abuse and neglect disgusted and enraged me. The idea that this could be tolerated by supposedly decent and responsible Church staff was beyond my comprehension.

The stories coming from disaffected public and staff were changing my view of what the Church of Scientology was about. There had been a time when I could have dismissed these allegations as a concerted effort to destroy the Church. But I'd come to realize there was no such effort going on except in the minds of Scientologists. Put simply, the Church was a victim of its own misdeeds. Through their over-zealousness and constant mishandling of its public, the Church was its own worst enemy. To compound matters, the Church continued to blame its problems on non-existent enemies and imaginary conspiracies.

In May 2002, I attended the annual Dianetics event at the San Jose Church. I wanted to get a first-hand glimpse of the latest goings on. It was the usual PR fluff I'd grown accustomed to. I sat through the video presentation, and stood up and politely clapped every time everybody else did. Scientology events always include a dozen or so standing ovations every time some accomplishment is announced or the name L. Ron Hubbard is mentioned. You get used to it.

Following the presentation, the lights came on and the evening's Master of Ceremonies stood before the crowd of about two hundred. He said as part of a new campaign to get more Dianetics and Scientology into the hands of the public, the San Jose org was urging all attendees to help distribute some of Hubbard's basic books into public hands. "Give these books to your family and friends," he announced.

As the announcement was made, a half a dozen staff began filtering through the crowd holding shiny red gift-bags, containing the Hubbard books. As they handed out the bags, the MC explained, "We're handing out these gift-bags to you so you can give the books to your family and friends."

One gift-bearing staff held out a bag to me and said, "Here you go."

I said, "What do you want me to do with that?"

He said, "Give them out to people."

I said, "Yeah, I guess I could do that." At that moment another staff member holding a receipt book approached me.

I asked innocently, "So you're just going to give me these books, so I can hand them out to people?" The book seller said, "No, you have to buy them."

I'd seen a lot of Scientology sales gimmicks in my time, but what a cheesy stunt this was. I rolled my eyes, shook my head, and walked out.

I haven't been inside a Scientology Church since.

My falling out with the Church was a gradual process, but I finally had to face some specific realities of my estrangement. I wouldn't be able to keep it a secret indefinitely. First off, I had no intention of ever taking another Scientology service. Eventually, someone would have to notice that. Second, the IAS would never see another penny of my money. That would definitely stand out.

Of greater concern was how to deal with Susie. I hadn't discussed with her in any detail what I'd been going through, although I'd dropped a few hints now and then. I wasn't sure how she might react to, "I think the Church of Scientology is a corrupt and incompetent organization. I'm not going to be a part of it anymore."

Common sense told me that given a choice between me and the Church, she'd side with me. But I couldn't be one hundred percent certain. I'd seen how easy it was for some Scientologists to sacrifice long standing relationships just so they could remain loyal to the Church. I'd seen how Scientologists reacted when the Church threatened to take away their "eternity." Expulsion meant never again having the chance of attaining total spiritual freedom. That threat could produce irrational responses and unfortunate consequences. I'd observed this in some of my own behavior, so I knew what I could be up against.

There was another problem. Susie and I were sufficiently prominent Scientologists so that Church management would want to intervene at the first sign of defection. I was concerned there'd be pressure put on us to reconsider, should we choose to resign from the Church. I didn't have any qualms about dealing with that kind of thing personally, but I wasn't sure how Susie would weather the sort of persuasion and "handling" the Church might impose on us.

Finally, I decided to stop wondering about all of the "what-ifs," and I started writing this book. I had so much going on in my mind that I thought the only way to explain it all would be to write it down in measured and sober detail. The more I wrote, the more I found I needed to keep writing. On one level it was a means of therapy, but somewhere within my experiences there seemed to be a story taking shape. If nothing else, it was my way of explaining to Susie my second thoughts concerning Scientology. It was also turning into a way of explaining the same thing to myself.

Now that I was in this new frame of mind, I decided to reinvent myself. I'd stay "on the inside" as long as I could and keep a record of the Church of Scientology's continuing exploits and publish my findings onto the Internet. It was a melodramatic posture, like I was the Green Hornet or something, but I liked the idea.

So in addition to working on my book, I started posting my views on the internet. My online pseudonym was Murray Luther, derived from Martin Luther, one of the principal leaders of the Protestant movement in the sixteenth century. Luther publicly opposed some of the policies of the Roman Papacy and proposed ways to reform a church he believed had become a corrupt organization.

I wasn't trying to equate my stature with that of Martin Luther, but I was a protester. I wanted to become a voice of dissent towards an established orthodoxy, and I felt compelled to speak my mind about it. At the same time I knew I'd have to do it anonymously or suffer instant retribution from the Church. And I liked my Murray Luther handle—as if I might have been Martin Luther's long lost cousin several times removed.

I contacted several Scientology critics who were well known on the internet. I wanted to start a regular online column from my perspective: a Scientologist, still in good standing, who was willing to speak out critically about the Church. After contacting a couple of critics via their web sites, I eventually found Kristi Wachter, a former Scientologist who maintains two web sites, *truthaboutscientology.com* and *scientology-lies.com*.

Her web material seemed straightforward and honest, and free from the hostile antagonism found on some anti-Scientology websites. I found a lot of the criticism on the internet to be distasteful, counter-productive, and just downright pointless. Kristi impressed me as pleasant, intelligent, and sincere about her desire to expose Church misbehavior. She certainly didn't fit the Church's profile of a Suppressive Person. There were a number of critics who I thought were decent and conscientious. What a different picture it was from the way such people were portrayed by the Church.

I proposed to Kristi a regular column that I'd write titled *The Regime Report* by Murray Luther. She thought it was a good idea, and said I could start submitting articles whenever I was ready. She even set up a Murray Luther index page that included a short bio and a nifty graphic that I created. Kristi has been unfailingly helpful, as well as enthusiastically supportive of my efforts. I hope I get the chance to thank her in person someday.

Although I'd stepped up my internet activities, I was still tentative about filling Susie in on the extent of what I'd been doing. As long as I continued my criticisms via the internet, the Church would sooner or later figure out my real identity. I hadn't gone to any great lengths to maintain my anonymity other than using a pseudonym, and I was well aware that any computer savvy person, with a little effort, could probably find out who I was. I didn't spend a lot of time worrying about it.

But by keeping my internet postings to myself, Susie would have plausible deniability in the event of any Church inquiry. I would bear the brunt of whatever pressure the Church might decide to put on me to cease my "anti-Scientology" activities. Unfortunately, I didn't take into account how all of this clandestine behavior would affect our relationship.

I'd become withdrawn and uncommunicative and Susie noticed. We hashed it out a few times and things would seem to improve slightly, but then it would turn sour again. I tried explaining, little by little, how my relationship with the Church was changing. I even mentioned that I had been doing a little browsing on the internet and had made a few contacts with ex-Scientologists. Susie seemed understanding, but only to a point. I thought the way I was dealing with my situation was making her a little uneasy.

One night, I showed Susie a website that had critical information about Scientology. I didn't ask her to read any of it, but only wanted to show her that such things existed. I wanted to point out that there was an unfavorable perception of Scientology that the Church had taken great pains to keep from its members. Then I showed her my *Regime Report* page on the *truthaboutscientology.com* website. Her reaction caught me by surprise. I probably should have seen it coming, but I'd misjudged the situation. She responded in both anger and fear. Angry, because I'd done something so bold without first consulting her, and fear of possible Church repercussions.

Susie's apprehension wasn't unwarranted. She knew what the Church and its members often resort to when they believe they're being threatened. She said, "I don't want to wake up one morning and find a bunch of Scientologists picketing in front of our house." It was a reasonable concern.

Some of the things I was going through are struggles that a lot of dissident Scientologists experience. For example, my difficulties wouldn't be limited to my marriage. Susie and I had a handful of very good Scientologist friends and scores of friendly acquaintances who were Church members. How was I going to deal with them? I could say nothing, and wait to be officially expelled by the Church. Once declared a Suppressive Person, Scientologists would be forbidden to have any contact with me. They'd even avoid mentioning my name. I would, in effect, disappear.

Chapter 25

On The Other Side

By 2003, I'd been sorting out my disagreements with Scientology for a couple of years. Susie was only beginning to deal with hers, and mostly because I kept bringing it up. I knew a time was coming when the Church would have to threaten us with expulsion. I think Susie was hoping that we might be able to just disappear quietly.

One day we talked about Scientologists who had left the Church, either through official expulsion or by their own choice. I lamented the policy that Scientologists are forbidden to have contact with such people. I brought up a friend we both knew from high school who became a Scientologist about a year after we did. Bob had written us a letter a couple of years earlier informing us he didn't want to be a Scientologist any more. Our reaction was typical of most Scientologists. We replied to him, each with our own letter, stating we wouldn't communicate with him anymore.

Although Church policy didn't explicitly require we disconnect from our friend under these circumstances, we sort of did the math on the situation and realized it would be impossible to maintain our relationship knowing that Bob had some fundamental disagreements. It was political expedience more than anything else that guided our decision.

Looking back, I was appalled at how easy it was to cut off a dear friend so dispassionately. I felt embarrassed, and I felt regret for having done something so cold. I'd been wrong, and now I wanted to make it right.

Susie said, "If that's the way you feel, then you should contact Bob."

It's exactly what I had in mind, and I felt encouraged that Susie agreed. I sent Bob an e-mail with a brief explanation and a link to my *Regime Report* website. I asked him to take a look at my essays and afterwards give me a call.

Several days later, Bob called our home and talked to Susie. She seemed pretty OK with it in spite of the ramifications it created with our relationship with the Church. I had a half-hour talk with him shortly after that, and we arranged a get together. We had a good time that weekend.

Bob was very familiar with the sort of "illicit" stories and reports I'd been uncovering on Scientology. He'd done a similar investigation a few years prior to mine, and had come to a similar conclusion about the Church. He urged Susie to read this "unapproved" material if she wanted a good understanding of my changing views about Scientology.

Susie had some reservations. Reading anything that puts the Church in an unfavorable light is one of the most taboo acts a Scientologist can commit. It's nearly equivalent to a Christian consorting with Satan. Scientologists close their eyes and turn away from all criticism lest they be corrupted by its evil. I suspect it's difficult for any Scientologist to break out of the mindset that compels you to close your eyes to other perspectives. Unfortunately, if you decide to open your eyes, you introduce the possibility of seeing something unpleasant.

Two months later, Susie and I again spent a couple of days with Bob. He brought along a few books, pamphlets, and assorted publications of Scientology related material—no doubt unauthorized by Church officials. He also brought a few electronic devices which I can only describe as variations of the E-meter. No question these devices were forbidden for Scientologists to mess around with.

The Church calls this sort of thing "squirrel" technology, something that's fairly prevalent outside of their orthodox world. A lot of ex-Scientologists have continued their practices without the Church's approval, and outside of their authority. The Church takes considerable efforts to prevent the dissemination and application of Scientology procedures that they don't monitor or control.

In any case, Susie and I allowed Bob to demonstrate his forbidden equipment, even to the extent of trying them out ourselves. We were engaging in Scientology's version of a blood-pact with the Devil. And now we possessed a dark secret we could never reveal to any Scientologist in good standing—unless, of course, we wanted to invoke the wrath of the Church. As melodramatic as it may sound, loyal Scientologists take this sort of thing very seriously. They know that any attempt to compromise the purity of the "Tech" will result in severe consequences.

■ **BACKGROUND:** Expulsion is the eventual fate of any Scientologist who refuses to cooperate with the Church. However, there are a number of preliminary actions the Church will take. In my case there'd be an initial attempt to get me to recant my blasphemy. Then I'd be asked to submit to a very thorough program supervised by the Ethics division. This would involve a confessional procedure by which I'd write up my "overts"—confessing my sins, in effect, and come clean on everything I said or did that was contrary to Church policy. I'd also be instructed to restudy a number of bulletins and policy letters to clear up my "misunderstandings." Finally, I'd be interrogated for the purpose of finding out where I'd gotten my unauthorized information. If this resembles the Spanish Inquisition, it's an apt comparison. ■

The rigorous procedures described above presuppose that I'd have some desire to reform my ungodly ways and get back in the good graces of the Church. But by this time, I couldn't have cared less what they thought about me.

I'd come to realize that the Church of Scientology was not the all-knowing, all-powerful center of wisdom I once thought it was. Toto had exposed the man behind the curtain, and now, the once awesome and fearsome power of the wizard had been reduced to theater shtick built on blustery stagecraft and over-the-top histrionics. How could I ever take the Church of Scientology seriously again?

Chapter 26

That Was Then, This is Now

"Men's courses will foreshadow certain ends, to which, if persevered in, they must lead, but if the courses be departed from, the ends will change."
— Charles Dickens, *A Christmas Carol*

All good stories need an ending. True stories, fiction, comedies, tragedies, adventures of any sort—there are no exceptions. We need closure, a conclusion, something substantial we can take with us as we leave the theater. I can't say with any certainty that my journey contains any of that. There was plenty of damage done, of that I'm certain. And while it's possible to recover from one's misfortunes, they can never be undone.

No one would disagree that we should learn from our mistakes, but it's not much of a lesson if it takes thirty years to get through it. Fool me twice, shame on me.

In between all of the turmoil there were plenty of good times. But I can't think of a single instance or event that had anything to do with my Church activities. Any memorable moment that I can recall revolved around friends and family, and I can't think of a single time that I would attribute any of it to Scientology.

The past can't be changed, but the future can. Though I wasn't able to escape the pressures, frustrations, and bitterness of my Scientology experiences, my children avoided a similar fate. How it happened, I'm not sure. Neither of them became Scientologists, nor did they ever express any real interest in it. And when we lived in LA, they were too young to be Sea Org recruiting material. So we probably moved to Monterey just in time. Just a few years later, two families we knew well each had a child join the Sea Org. I'm glad we never had to go through that.

Susie and I never discussed it much, but neither of us ever made any serious effort to get them involved in Scientology. I've sometimes wondered why. Maybe it was the cost involved. It was all we could do to keep up with our own Church expenses. Maybe we were waiting for them to become old enough to make their own choices. And there was that Illegal PC thing still hanging over our heads. Our kids would likely inherit that baggage. Whatever the reason, we never had a specific plan for raising them as Scientologists.

I've sometimes wondered if I might have had another reason. Occasionally, I've speculated that maybe I had some unconscious, sub-conscious, or otherwise intuitive impulse to keep them from getting involved in the sort of stressful situations that I knowingly and willingly put up with for half of my life. On some level, maybe my better instincts prevailed. All I know for sure is that Susie and I were extremely lucky that our children never turned into devoted Church members. Call it providence if you like.

I don't remember the exact moment, but one day it dawned on me that my kids would very likely never find themselves in the cruel clutches of Scientology. Realizing that has given me peace of mind and an absolution that my former Church could never provide. I'm proud of the way they've turned out. But more than that, I have a deep satisfaction that they've succeeded in life without Scientology's aggressive and intrusive interference. For that I've been thankful.

Scientologists will come and go, but family will always remain.

It's been over a decade since the original writing of this book. In all of that time neither Susie nor I have received any official Church declaration of our status or lack thereof. Needless to say, I've lost touch with my Scientologist friends, with the exception of two who left the Church like me.

For several years I got lots of mail and phone calls from various Church organizations. There were many efforts to get me and Susie back on the Bridge, but it wasn't going to happen. Eventually, I started telling any Scientologist who might ask that I didn't consider myself a Scientologist anymore. That was enough to put an end to the mail and phone calls. And I suspect the Church may have known about my Murray Luther alter-ego, though I believe for the most part I'd been cruising beneath their radar. For all I know, somewhere along the line I've been declared a Suppressive Person. It's not unusual for the Church to issue such declarations without informing the recipient.

In spite of Susie's misgivings about Church repercussions, she nevertheless felt deeply betrayed by their decision to reinstate her Illegal PC status. I can only guess as to how she'll eventually come through all of it. She might have to write her own book.

In Scientology, my existence revolved around Scientology principles. Everything I experienced or accomplished was within that context. It's taken me a while to start thinking outside of that box.

I've walked away with at least one thing that I might not have acquired if I hadn't been a Scientologist for so many years. I've gotten inoculated from manipulative propaganda. I subscribe to no ideologies, nor do I carry a torch for any leader, be it political, religious, or social. I've become an independent thinker who doesn't need to consult an ideological treatise in order make a decision, craft an opinion, or solve a problem.

Getting locked in to an ideology can make smart people fall for stupid ideas. And the Church of Scientology is hardly the only organization that uses manipulative tactics to forward theirs. I've come to understand the anatomy and mindset of the ideological zealot. You can find them everywhere in all walks of life. Each and every one of them has some kind of utopian vision they believe will bring about a better world. For them, no end is greater, and therefore no means too severe. These are the followers of religious movements, political action, and social revolutions. These are society's true believers who are convinced that they know a better way. Unfortunately, their way almost always comes at a high cost, and brings about dubious results.

I don't consider myself a religious person in any conventional sense. I do have my own spiritual concepts but I have no need or desire to explain or defend them. They're mine, and mine alone. Though I'm no longer an evangelist, please allow me one last moment to stand up on my soapbox to preach the gospel of Pete Townshend, guitarist for the Who, and also one of my favorite songwriters.

> *"I'll tip my hat to the new constitution*
> *Take a bow for the new revolution*
> *Smile and grin at the change all around*
> *Pick up my guitar and play*
> *Just like yesterday*
> *Then I'll get on my knees and pray*
> *We don't get fooled again."*

Epilogue

On Sunday Feb 18, 2018, I decided to take a trip to one of the Scientology Churches in my area. It was a big event to unveil their latest "Ideal Org" in Mountain View, CA. Even though the last time I set foot in a Church of Scientology was way back in 2002, I wanted to check it out.

I'd seen the latest Scientology TV commercial titled, "Curious?" that appeared during the Super Bowl broadcast and later on in the Winter Olympics. It occurred to me that I was indeed curious.

I wasn't even sure if they'd let me in. All big events are heavily policed by their own security detail, and I wasn't sure how much info they had on me in their member database. But I decided to play it straight, and see what would happen.

The street that led to the entrance was blocked off by two police cars and two patrol officers. It's standard for the Church to enlist assistance from local law enforcement. The police always seem to cooperate.

Scientology security personnel were everywhere, coordinating their patrols using walkie-talkies. Leader of the Church, David Miscavige was going to be there, and he always gets the Secret Service treatment.

As I arrived, there were two rows of tables with staff screening the incoming attendees. I approached the first row and was given a card to fill out: name, address, phone, training and auditing level, and a brief checkbox questionnaire asking about my future plans as an active Scientologist. Pretty standard stuff. I filled out my name, gave an e-mail address, and my training and auditing level.

I turned it in, and the event lady asked, "Address and phone number?" I'd left those blank. I asked, "Is that information mandatory?" Apparently it was a question she wasn't qualified to answer. I was taken to the next row of tables.

I was now dealing with the next level of their security process: event staff with computers and cell phones. The lady entered my name in the computer and it didn't look like anything came up. I explained, "I hesitate to give out my address and phone number because then I get a lot of phone calls and emails." I wasn't trying to make trouble. I was just stating a fact from past experience. The lady seemed annoyed at my candor.

I could tell that the event staff were well drilled. Miscavige would be appearing, after all, so I knew I was dealing with the "A" team from the security arm of Scientology's Office of Special Affairs. I was cool and casual.

The lady asked, "Do you have your ID number?" "ID number?" I queried. I wasn't sure what she meant. "Your license," she said. OSA intelligence can be pretty slick when it wants to be, but I thought the risk was minimal. The address on my license wasn't current and there was no phone number.

The lady entered my license number into the computer and it didn't seem to produce a result. I wondered, "Are Scientologists really given an identification number these days?" I'd never heard of such a thing. She pointed to a table that was off to the side and said, "You'll need to talk to Ryan. Tell him that I sent you." "OK," I thought, "I'm advancing to the next level of their security protocols."

So I met Ryan, and he had me wait at his table while he talked to the lady. They were contacting someone via cell phone, and I'm sure they didn't want me within earshot of the conversation.

Then a lady I hadn't seen before walked past me about ten yards in front. Clearly dressed in security-type wear (formal, but official), she surreptitiously took a picture of me with a concealed device of some sort. I pretended like I didn't notice.

After a couple of minutes, yet another security lady walked up to me. "Are you Chris?" I said yes, and she immediately began to deliver her report. But I interrupted her, "And you are?" I was trying to be nice. She was trying to be intimidating.

I'm sure she'd drilled this kind of encounter numerous times. Her patter was dour, curt, and devoid of human feeling. "You're not allowed into the event," she said without an ounce of sympathy or regret.

Still playing it straight and innocent, I asked, "Am I not in your database?" In a similarly innocent way she answered, "You'll need to contact Ethics." There was no way I was going to get an explanation more detailed than that. I'll play it innocent, but I won't play it stupid. I knew what she meant and I assumed she knew that I knew. The only person within the Church that I'd be allowed to speak to was an Ethics Officer. About the only thing left to say was, "OK, thanks for letting me know." I turned and left.

As I was driving home I thought, "Well, if I wasn't in their database before, I certainly was in it now." The experiment was complete. It was like one of those old David Letterman routines: "Can a man in a bear suit order a sandwich at the corner deli?" Except in my case it was, "Can a disaffected former Scientologist walk into one of their public events?" I can attest firsthand that the answer is no.

Glossary

Advanced Organization of Los Angeles, is where the OT Levels I through V are delivered.

American Saint Hill Organization, named after L. Ron Hubbard's home in East Grinstead, Sussex, England, and once the world wide headquarters of Scientology. ASHO delivers the *Saint Hill Special Briefing Course*, a long and comprehensive course for student auditors.

Auditing, the processes and procedures of Dianetics and Scientology applied to the individual with the goal of raising the person's awareness and abilities.

The Bridge, the route to Clear; also known as the "route to total freedom; in general use means the complete line up of auditing and training steps.

Class IV, technical designation of a Church of Scientology Central Organization. It corresponds with the Class IV auditor's certification, the highest level of training and auditing a Class IV Org can deliver.

Clear, is the goal of Dianetics processing; A Clear is knowingly at cause over mental matter, energy, space and time; a Clear is free from irrational thoughts and feelings.

Clearing, in a collective sense, is the combined activities that are supposedly bringing sanity to the world using the techniques of Scientology.

Committee of Evidence, a fact finding body put together to investigate various problems and difficulties that might occur within a Church organization.

Dianetics, mental therapy developed by L. Ron Hubbard. He called it a "science of the mind."

E-meter, an electronic instrument used by the auditor to aid in Dianetics and Scientology processing. The auditor uses the E-meter to determine what to audit and monitor the progress of auditing processes.

Ethics, also Department of Ethics, that section of a Church organization that ensures that Scientology is being properly applied.

Ethics Conditions, a scale that denotes the state of any activity in terms of degree of success or failure.

Fifth Invader Force, Hubbard claims that ancient Egypt was the site of a galactic conflict between the Fourth and Fifth invader forces, also known as the Space Command and the Martian Command.

Field Staff Member, a sales rep for the Church who operates in a freelance fashion and makes money off of commissions from services paid. FSMs are not contracted staff members.

Flag, the Church of Scientology's headquarters where OT VII is delivered. Flag promotes itself as the Mecca of technical perfection where auditing and training is flawlessly delivered.

Freewinds, also called the Flagship Org, and colloquially known as "the Ship," is a cruise ship based in Aruba, in the Netherlands Antilles; responsible for delivering OT VII.

Guardians Office, Branch of the Church that once handled legal affairs and public relations for the Church. In the early 80's it was disbanded and replaced with the Office of Special Affairs.

HGC, short for Hubbard Guidance Center, it's the department of any Church organization where Scientology auditing occurs.

Implant, an electronic means of controlling a thetan. It's considered both malicious and harmful.

Mission, is a Scientology organization granted the right to deliver elementary Scientology and Dianetics services.

Office of Special Affairs, formerly the Guardians Office, OSA was organized following the GO's legal problems in the late 70's and early 80's. They handle the Church's legal and public relations issues.

OT, short for operating thetan; it describes a spiritual being who is able to operate independently of a physical (human) body; ideally, an OT has cause over life, thought, matter, energy, space and time. (see also *thetan*)

OT V, auditing classification one receives after completing the New Era Dianetics for OTs auditing program.

OT VIII, auditing classification where one reaches the state of "Truth Revealed." It is currently the highest auditing level a Scientologist can achieve.

PC, short for preclear; in popular usage it refers to anyone receiving auditing.

Postulate, in Scientology usage is a mental determination meant to initiate, change, or stop some condition or action.

PTS , potential trouble source; someone connected to a suppressive person or group. (*see suppressive person*)

Reactive Mind, the unconscious portion of the mind that causes irrational behavior, unwanted emotions, and psychosomatic illnesses.

Religious Technology Center, arm of the Church that owns all of Scientology's trade and service marks, and controls their use through licensing. The RTC's stated purpose is to protect Scientology and ensure its proper application.

Scientology, Hubbard called it the "science of knowing." He claimed that it produces greater awareness, intelligence and ability; through Scientology one is supposed to be able to achieve immortality.

Security Check, Sec Check for short, is a type of process done on the e-meter to discover specific things a Scientologist might have thought or done that could be considered detrimental to the Church.

Session, short for auditing session.

Squirrel, someone who alters Scientology procedure or uses it without proper Church authorization.

Suppressive Person, as designated by an Ethics Officer, one who tries to harm Scientology or Scientologists; In general, anyone who is continuously committing, harmful acts. (*see Ethics*)

Thetan, the spirit as designated by Hubbard; it is essentially who you are as a unique individual; a thetan can survive independent of a human body.

Training, instruction in the delivery of Scientology procedures, which can include the application of the administrative policies and procedures of the Church organization.

References

All entries are by L. Ron Hubbard except where otherwise indicated.

Chapter 1
1 – HCOPL "Illegal PC's, Acceptance of High Crime PL," 6 Dec.
   1976RB
2 – RJ 67 (audio taped message, Sept. 1967)
3 – RJ 34 "The Future of Scientology" Mar. 13, 1982
4 – Video interview with Tory Christman, Aug. 22, 2000 *Xenu TV*

Chapter 3
1 – HCOPL "Keeping Scientology Working," 7 Feb. 65
2 – HCOPL "Handling of Resign-up Refusals, 4 Dec 71 II
3 – *Scientology, the Fundamentals of Thought*, 1975,
4 – *Introduction to Scientology Ethics*, 1989, "Disconnection,"

Chapter 4
1 – *History of Man*, 1968
2 – HCOPL "Keeping Scientology Working," 7 Feb. 65

Chapter 5
1 – HCOPL "Scientology Five; Press Policies," 14 Aug. 63
2 – HCOPL "Keeping Scientology Working," 7 Feb. 65
3 – IGN Bulletin No. 44 "Wake Up Call," 11 Sep 01

Chapter 7

1 – LRH ED 284 INT 16 Sept. 1976, "The Solution to Inflation"
2 – *Scientology 0-8 – The Book of Basics*, 1975
3 – Orders of the Day, 25 Dec. 1976

Chapter 8
1 – HCOPL "Leaving and Leaves," 7 Dec. 1976

Chapter 10
1 – HCOPL "Suppressive Acts," 23 Dec. 1965
2 – HCOPL "Cancellation of Fair Game," 21 Oct. 1968

Chapter 12
2 – RJ 34 "The Future of Scientology" Mar. 13, 1982

Chapter 14
1 – HCOPL "Illegal PC's, Acceptance of High Crime PL," 6 Dec. 1976RB

Chapter 22
1 – HCOPL "Handling of Resign-up Refusals, 4 Dec 71 II

Chapter 24
1 – IGN Bulletin No. 44 "Wake Up Call," 11 Sep 01

Abbreviation Notes:
HCOPL – Hubbard Communication Office Policy Letter
IGN – Inspector General's Network
LRH ED – L. Ron Hubbard Executive Directive
RJ – Ron's Journal

Subject Index

Made in the USA
Middletown, DE
24 August 2018